ROAD BIKING™

Northern California

Help Us Keep This Guide Up to Date

Every effort has been made by the author and editors to make this guide as accurate and useful as possible. However, many things can change after a guide is published—roads are closed, regulations change, techniques evolve, facilities come under new management, etc.

We would love to hear from you concerning your experiences with this guide and how you feel it could be improved and kept up to date. While we may not be able to respond to all comments and suggestions, we'll take them to heart and we'll also make certain to share them with the author. Please send your comments and suggestions to the following address:

The Globe Pequot Press
Reader Response/Editorial Department
P.O. Box 480
Guilford, CT 06437

Or you may e-mail us at:

editorial@globe-pequot.com

Thanks for your input, and happy travels!

ROAD BIKING™ SERIES

A **FALCON** GUIDE ®

ROAD BIKING ™

Northern California

Road Rides for the Serious Cyclist

THIRD EDITION

John Nagiecki
and
Kimberly Grob

FALCON®

Guilford, Connecticut
An imprint of The Globe Pequot Press

Photos by John Nagiecki unless otherwise noted
Text design by Lesley Weissman-Cook
Maps by Tim Kissel

Library of Congress Cataloging-in-Publication Data is available.

ISBN 0-7627-1192-2

Manufactured in the United States of America
Third Edition/First Printing

To Siri,
For doing all you did while I worked on the book.

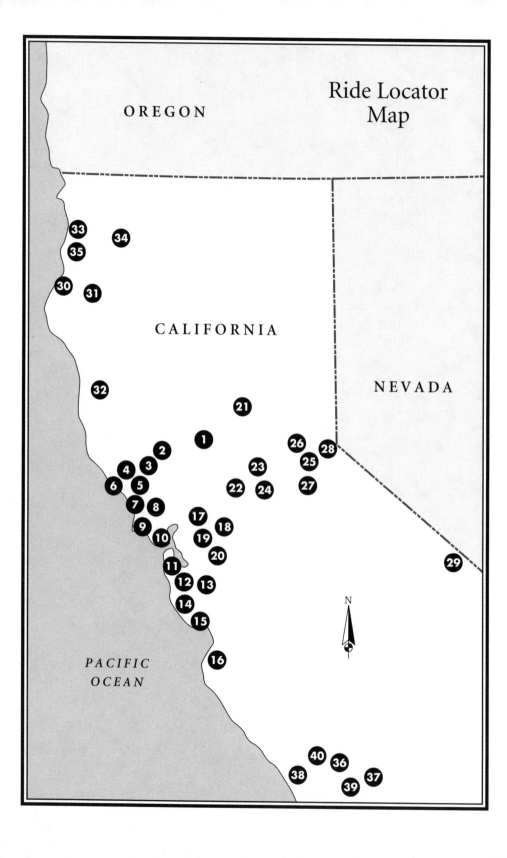

Contents

Preface

To ride a bicycle properly is very much like a love affair—chiefly it is a matter of faith. Believe you can do it, and the thing is done; doubt, and, for the life of you, you cannot.

— H. G. WELLS, *WHEELS OF CHANCE,* 1896

Among his many passions novelist H. G. Wells loved to bicycle and often went on rides through the English countryside on a tandem with his wife. Looking back on that golden age of bicycling, it's difficult to imagine how Wells and the large lot of his contemporaries rode those clunky, single-speed machines, with braking that relied mostly on luck and a prayer. Yet somehow they did, in knickerbocker suits and skirts, some riding the new-found freedom of their "wheel" as far as they could go.

Though technology has made pedaling easier, the simple joy of riding hasn't changed. Beyond the gilded frames and shiny components, bicycling is still about riding in the open air by the power of one's legs and lungs. It's a sensuous journey in which we respond physically and emotionally to the challenge of the land. And like the love affair that Wells compares it to, it is not only extraordinarily pleasing but sometimes painful and difficult.

I've had some of the finest and some of the worst moments of my life on a bicycle. The worst moments all involved terrible crashes, where I either broke, bruised, or burned some part of my body. I can remember vowing never to go near another bike. But I recovered my nerve and now gladly retell the more spectacular falls in all their gory detail and at the slightest provocation.

I could say that my finest moments involved cresting the summit of a long, winding grade to catch the glint of the distant ocean or gliding down a mountain for seemingly endless miles, but that wouldn't be accurate. The truth is that my finest bicycling moments all had to do with the people I have met. One of the more memorable times involved an extended tour down the Pacific coast several summers ago. Along the way I met up with other cyclists from Canada, England, Germany, and different states, all of us heading south to California. We rode and camped together in hiker-biker sites, climbed tough hills, ducked rain, soaked up sun, and enjoyed some of the most spectacular scenery on earth. It was a magical time, one that I will never forget, especially since one of the group eventually became my wife.

So as you venture out onto the road and explore the routes in this book, remember that every ride is a small leap of faith. Believe not only that you can do the ride you set out to do, but also that you may encounter one of the finer moments of your life. Of course, if it doesn't happen on today's ride, there's always the next, and the next, and the next after that. Along the way there will likely be lessons learned, so stick with it. Remember, as proper bicycling is very much like a love affair, so too is proper loving very much like a bicycle ride— chiefly it is a matter of endurance. Stay in the saddle!

—John Nagiecki

Acknowledgments

Many individuals have made this book possible. First and foremost I want to thank all the people at the various bike shops mentioned in this book who unwittingly answered the phone when I called. Thank you all for taking the time out to get the information I needed. Other helpful folks include the staff at the Foresthill Ranger Station, the East Bay Regional Parks Department, and the Marin French Cheese Company, as well as Bob Anderson of the Alpine County Chamber of Commerce and Ed McLaughlin of the Chico Velo Cycling Club, all of whom graciously responded to my pesky questions and requests. I also want to thank Kimberly Grob, who wrote *Best Bike Rides Northern California,* which served as the basis for this book, and John Elgart, who revised the second edition. Many thanks also to Jeff Serena and Jan Cronan for their editorial assistance and kind criticism, Lesley Weissman-Cook for her wonderful design, and the rest of the staff at Globe Pequot for their first-rate professional contributions. I also want to thank my wife, Siri Ming, who deserves special recognition both for being Canadian and for braving the California heat while accompanying me on the rides in this book. Thanks also for keeping my prose in line whenever it started to wander.

What bicycling is really all about. Café in downtown San Luis Obispo on the San Luis Valley Cruise.

Introduction

Think of this book as an old, weathered cycling friend. The one who's been around the proverbial block a few times. This buddy of yours will take you on a sampling of favorite rides, but in the long run you'll find your own variation and come up with your own list of primo routes.

This book is not a bible or an encyclopedia; it's merely a starting point, a launching pad for your own adventures. It's meant to be a trusty resource, reliable guide, and faithful friend. Those who get the most out of its pages will be bold enough to build upon the suggestions it offers.

Most of the rides in this book wind through rural areas, generally following loop routes. Most also begin in a town, a city, or some other central location, and several follow loops through the heart of an urban area. Whether in rural or urban terrain, you will be exploring areas with which you are likely to be somewhat if not totally unfamiliar. Take heed: riding a bike into unknown parts can be a considerable challenge, requiring you to be ever watchful of where you are, how far you've come, and what's expected ahead. Vigilance is the best defense against getting off the prescribed track.

It's a good idea to thoroughly study the route before setting out on the road, so that you have a good sense of the lay of the land, frequency of turns, major landmarks, etc. And once out on the road, take your time, and stop often to check your directions and map (never read directions while riding your bike). I highly recommend that you get a good road map of the area and carry it along. That way you'll be able to navigate around unexpected road construction, get yourself back on track when lost, or discover new roads to ride. A local county map is a good place to start. Other options include topographic maps or a cycling-specific map, such as those produced by Krebs Cycle Products. (For more information on this and other resources, see the Appendix in the back of this book.)

HOW TO USE THIS BOOK

The forty rides in this book range from the long-distance hilly variety to flat and short spins. To help you match the ride level with your ability, experience, attitude, or mood, we've classified them into four groups based on their length and terrain. But don't get hung up on the definitions. What we call a "ramble" may seem more like a "classic" to a beginner, and the gonzoloids may laugh at some of the rides we call "challenges." No matter what, some rides will be on

the borderline, so it's always best to pull out a good map to make your own assessment. Also, while most of the rides are suited to standard road-biking equipment, there are a few where cyclecross or mountain bike equipment might be desired, due to rough road conditions or brief trail riding. If you ride your road bike on nothing other than the road, consider taking another style of bike on one of these rides.

Whale Rock Reservoir and the distant Pacific from Old Creek Road on the Cambria Challenge.

Rambles are the most basic of rides, accessible to almost all riders. They can be easily completed in one day and follow flat to slightly rolling terrain and cover less than 35 miles.

Cruises are intermediate in difficulty and distance. They are generally 25 to 50 miles long and may include some moderate climbs and descents. An experienced rider can easily complete a cruise in one day, but inexperienced or less fit riders may want to take two days, with an overnight stop.

Challenges are difficult and suited to experienced riders in good condition. Beginning riders who take on a challenge may find themselves cursing the road, this book, and life in general halfway through a ride. These routes are tough. They are usually 40 to 60 miles long and include steep climbs and descents. Water and food may not be available, requiring you to bring adequate supplies along.

Classics are the most difficult rides in this book. They are typically 60 miles in length or longer and include tough climbs and descents. They may take you far away from such civilized needs as water or food and thus require you to carefully plan ahead. Tackle them only if you are fit and comfortable in the hinterlands on a lonely road.

So which ride or rides are for you? It depends. Feel like trying to initiate a friend into the sport? Go for an ultrascenic ramble. Experiencing the need to hammer your brains out and proclaim your virility? There are a few classics in here that will give your bad-assed, big-legged body the thrashing it so dearly desires—just be sensible about it and don't exceed your own limits. Of course, most of the rides are somewhere in between these two extremes.

Fog rolls in over Muir Woods Road on the Bolinas Challenge.

GETTING THE MOST OUT OF YOUR RIDE

There are reams of articles, papers, and books on cycling. Just on the subject of smart and safe riding techniques, stacks of articles and books have been written, all of which have contributed to preventing untold numbers of misfortunes and accidents. They cover everything from the proper way to cross railroad tracks and manage dog dangers to doing a bike-safety check and making yourself visible to traffic. Even if you know it all, at least refamiliarize yourself with the safety literature. And while collecting and absorbing written advice will improve your riding tremendously, don't forget that the miles in the saddle are what really make the cyclist. Learning to ride intelligently—and to ride with grace, etiquette, and class—is a continual process of education and experience. There's always more to learn.

Cyclo-journalists and their cycling advice have been around since the invention of two wheels. In the spirit of the pioneers, I offer the following credo developed in the late 1800s by a respected writer and rider named Velocio (Paul de Vivie). It covers the basics and is as relevant today as it was then.

Velocio's Commandments

- Stop briefly and not too often, so as not to chill or lose your rhythm.
- Eat frequently and lightly, eat before you are hungry, and drink before you are thirsty.
- Don't push yourself until you are too tired to eat or sleep.
- Add clothing before you are cold, take it off before you are hot, but don't avoid sun, air, and rain.
- Avoid alcohol and meat, at least while on the road.
- Ride within your limits. Learn your pace, and don't be tempted to force yourself during the first hours of a ride, when you are fresh.
- Don't show off (ride out of vanity).

And to this I add a modern-day addendum: Always wear a helmet. Though there has been some debate on the Internet of late as to the efficacy of helmets, it is not worth getting into. Think of your helmet as your personal safety statement. As you ride down the road, it is the banner you wear that says, "I am riding responsibly," a slogan we should all repeat to ourselves as we pedal along.

Wine Country

Middletown Cruise

MIDDLETOWN — HARBIN HOT SPRINGS —
LOCH LOMAND — MIDDLETOWN

Beyond the hubbub of the Napa Valley is a quiet landscape where native oaks and grasses prevail, and small, circuitous two-lanes snake up tall hills. Middletown, a crossroads in this untrammeled area of Lake County, can sometimes feel more like Montana than it does California, with its big, wide-open sky and mix of ranchers and sportsmen rambling through town.

But there is another frontier here—the New Age kind—that makes this a quintessential California kind of place. The natural peace of the area is perfect for meditation, and several retreat centers cater to those in search of a higher spiritual consciousness. Among the more renowned is Harbin Hot Springs, a clothing-optional, 1,200-acre resort run by the Heart Consciousness Church, a New Age group advocating holistic health and spiritual renewal. Aside from photographers, drinkers, and gawkers, anyone is welcome at Harbin, as long as you pay the entrance fee. It's a wonderful place where you can meditate, take a yoga class, soak in one of several naturally heated pools, enjoy a vegetarian meal, or relax on a large deck (bring lots of sun block). You can be a day visitor until 9:00 P.M., camp, or have a room with a bath. Room reservations are suggested. Contact Harbin Hot Springs, P.O. Box 782, Middletown, CA 95461; (707) 987–2477.

While topless or naked cycling certainly wouldn't turn many heads on Harbin's property, clothing is highly recommended for the outlying country

Two wheels on Big Canyon Road north of Middletown.

Start: Main Street (Highway 29) and Highway 175 in Middletown.

Length: 29.4 miles.

Terrain: Rolling, with extended climbing and lengthy descents. Few flats. Mostly rural roads, with light to moderate traffic areas.

Food: An all-purpose convenience store and a health-food store are located in Middletown, along with a brewery (that serves food) and several restaurants. A small grocery and grill bar are located at Loch Lomond. Harbin Hot Springs has a restaurant, which serves breakfast and dinner and has a coffee cafe and a general store.

For more information: Palisades Mountain Sport, 1330 B Gerrard Street, Calistoga, CA 94515; (707) 942–9687.

Maps: DeLorme *Northern California Atlas and Gazetteer*, maps 83 and 84; Compass Maps, *Napa and Lake Counties.*

roads. Though this borderline cruise is short in distance, it is amply supplied in steep, long climbs and descents. If you're not a hill climber (or descender), this ride is not for you.

The cruise leaves Middletown (1,100 feet) on flat, but bumpy, Barnes Road and soon climbs up the first short hill to the Harbin Hot Springs Road turnoff. But you'll have to put off the Harbin scene for now and instead expand your mind and lungs on Big Canyon Road. You'll roll up and down for nearly 3 miles along Big Canyon, where passing cars are about as rare as spotted owls in Oregon (but don't get too comfortable, a vehicle always comes unheard and unseen around a blind corner). After about 5 miles into this cruise, the road begins to go up much more than it goes down. At 10 miles it goes steadily up a set of switchbacks that hang on the edge of a rocky hillside, offering wonderful views of the canyon and surrounding hills.

You then traverse a high valley passing the Hoberg Airfield (a dirt runway) before turning onto Loch Lomond Road. Vehicles again appear on Loch Lomond Road, so flick the traffic-wary devices back on in your brain. The climbing begins almost immediately and, with a few brief interruptions, goes on for 2 miles. At times it is breathtakingly steep and can leave you wobbly. At the final summit, over 3,000 feet, you can sometimes experience snow or sleet during the colder months.

Loch Lomond, named for the tiny nearby lake, has a small store and grill bar, but not much else. This is where you join Highway 175, which takes you back to Middletown. At this point you may be wondering, "What about the payback for all that climbing?" Not yet. You still have a little more up before the big descent.

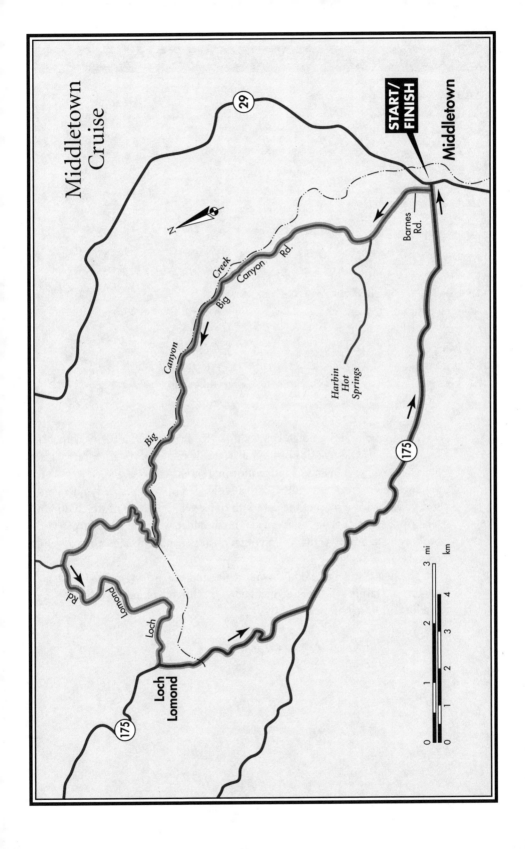

Middletown Cruise

START/FINISH

Middletown

29

N

Big Canyon Creek

Big Canyon Rd.

Barnes Rd.

Harbin Hot Springs

175

Loch Lomond Rd.

Loch Lomond

175

3 mi

km

0   1   2   3   4

0.0 Head west on Highway 175.

0.1 Right onto Barnes Road, following Harbin Hot Springs Retreat Center sign.

1.2 Begin moderate climb.

1.6 Summit. Bear right onto Big Canyon Road and begin descending. (Turnoff for Harbin Hot Springs to left.)

2.2 Bottom of descent. Begin rolling hills.

5.3 Begin gradual climb.

10.2 Begin switchback climb.

11.5 Summit.

13.2 Left toward Loch Lomond on Loch Lomond Road.

13.7 Begin steep climb.

15.1 Summit. Begin rolling hills (more up than down).

17.3 Loch Lomond. Turn left onto Highway 175.

17.8 Begin gradual climb.

19.1 Summit. Begin steep descent.

26.2 Bottom of hill.

29.3 Ride ends at intersection with Highway 29 at stoplight in Middletown.

The traffic is also a notch heavier on 175. Given the number of churches located on this Old Age side of the valley, traffic can be particularly heavy just after Saturday-evening and Sunday-morning services.

Your reward begins at mile 19. It's advisable to keep your speed under control, as you will be sharing the lane with other vehicles, some of which do not take kindly to cyclists on "their" road. The shoulder, what there is of it, can also be dicey, with drainage ditches and other obstacles suddenly appearing around corners.

The final 3 miles to Middletown are flat and fast. Afterward it's time for a soak up at Harbin—if you're so inclined— in a tub full of naked people, before heading off to rejoin the world.

Dry Creek and Alexander Valleys Ramble

HEALDSBURG — DRY CREEK — GEYSERVILLE — CHIANTI —
ASTI — DRY CREEK — HEALDSBURG

I *magine rolling through vineyards on your bicycle, stopping at wineries to sample their best vintage, picnicking under a shady oak, all the while basking in the mellow Mediterranean climate. Sound good? It is. And it's right here in the Dry Creek and Alexander Valleys.*

This ramble takes you through the heart of one of Sonoma County's premier wine-growing regions, a bucolic wonderland where sun and soil conspire to produce some of the most sublime flavors ever squeezed from a grape. Unlike the more mainstream wine destinations in Napa and Sonoma, however, the Dry Creek and Alexander Valleys are still relatively quiet and lightly traveled.

The ramble begins in the town of Healdsburg,

Cruising past olive trees and vines on Asti Road in the Alexander Valley.

Start: Intersection of Center and Plaza Streets on the northeast corner of Healdsburg's downtown plaza.

Length: 32.8 miles.

Terrain: Flat, with two moderate climbs and several gentle rolling hills.

Food: Downtown Healdsburg has a good selection of bistros and cafes. A general store is located at the intersection of Dry Creek and Lambert Bridge Roads.

For more information: Spoke Folk Cyclery, 249 Center Street, Healdsburg, CA; (707) 433–7171.

Maps: DeLorme *Northern California Atlas and Gazetteer,* map 83; Krebs Cycle Products, *North San Francisco Bay and Wine Country* map.

whose green, shady square is surrounded by cafes, book and antiques shops, and gourmet restaurants. Cyclists often congregate on the square on weekend mornings, sipping double lattes before wandering off into vineland. Healdsburg can be a busy place at times, but after only a mile and a half, you'll be out of the residential area and into the country on Dry Creek Road, the main artery through the valley. During harvest season in late summer and early fall, trucks overflowing with bunches of grapes may hurry past you on their way to the crushing plant. The stains that you see on the road, which can be as slippery as motor oil, are the remains of some of their cargo, which slipped through the cracks.

At 4.7 miles you'll pass the Dry Creek General Store. This isn't a Disney re-creation, but a real old-time general store that looks as though it's been there forever. Soon afterward at mile 8.4, you turn on Canyon Road and begin one of the few climbs of the trip, which takes you out of the Dry Creek and into the Alexander Valley. (To cut 14 miles off this ride, continue straight on Dry Creek Road for another 0.2 mile to Yoakim Bridge Road, where you will turn left. Continue with the directions given below that begin at mile 23.)

Once out of the hills and back in the vines, you follow frontage roads through the valley along Highway 101, crossing under twice. The views to the west are of the Mayacamas Mountains, the tallest of which is Mount St. Helena at 4,344 feet. At mile 16.8 you turn onto Dutcher Creek Road and begin the return climb to the Dry Creek Valley, entering at its far northern end. In the hills to the right, you can catch a glimpse of the spillway for the Warm Springs Dam, which created Lake Sonoma and, in turn, made the valley a little bit shorter.

At mile 22.4 you turn right on Yoakim Bridge Road and then left on West Dry Creek Road. The latter is quite narrow and skirts beneath shady hillsides

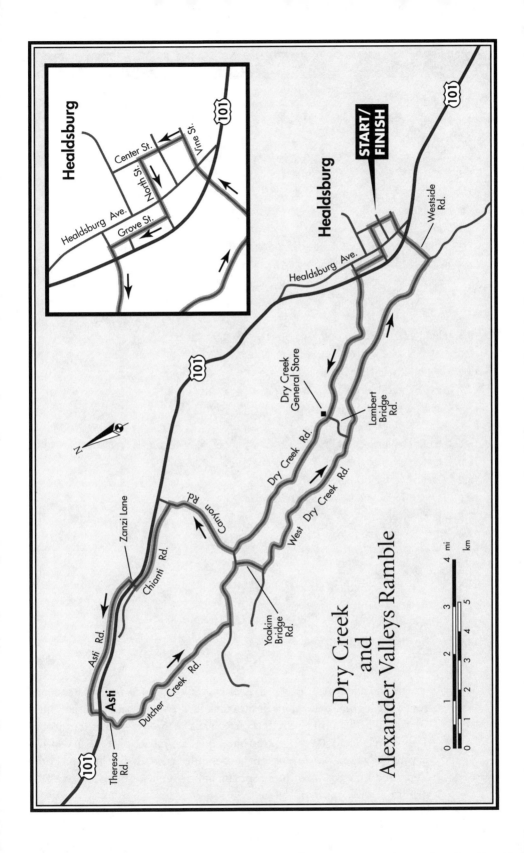

Dry Creek
and
Alexander Valleys Ramble

0.0 Head north on Center Street for one block. Turn left on North Street.

0.1 Follow North Street across Healdsburg Avenue at traffic light.

0.2 Right at stop sign onto Grove Street.

0.6 Continue straight at stop-sign intersection with Grant Street.

1.3 Left on Dry Creek Road at traffic light. Busy area; ride with caution.

1.4 Continue straight on Dry Creek Road under Highway 101. Good shoulder begins.

4.7 Continue straight on Dry Creek Road at stop-sign intersection with Lambert Bridge Road. Pass Dry Creek General Store on right. Shoulder narrows.

8.4 Right on Canyon Road. Begin gradual climb. (For a shorter ride continue straight to Yoakim Bridge Road and turn left. Resume directions at mile 23.0 below).

10.1 Summit. Pass Olive Hill Cemetery on right. Begin short, steep descent.

10.6 Left on Chianti Road (before Highway 101 underpass).

10.8 Pass Geyser Peak Winery on left.

13.2 Right on Zanzi Lane. Ride 100 yards, cross under Highway 101, and turn left onto Asti Road.

15.3 Continue straight on Asti Road at stop-sign intersection with Asti P.O. Road. Pass Asti Winery on right.

16.5 Left onto unmarked Theresa Road. Cross under Highway 101.

16.8 Left onto Dutcher Creek Rd. Terrain moderately rolling.

18.2 Begin steady, moderate climb.

18.6 Summit. Begin long, gradual descent.

20.9 Left onto Dry Creek Road.

22.4 Right onto Yoakim Bridge Road.

23.0 Left onto West Dry Creek Road.

31.6 Left on Westside Road.

32.3 Cross under Highway 101. Enter Healdsburg.

32.5 Cross Healdsburg Avenue at traffic light. Continue straight on Vine Street.

32.6 Left on Center Street (Spoke Folk Cyclery on left).

32.8 End Center and Plaza Streets.

and past an assortment of wineries. It will take you to West Side Road, and from there it's only a few spins of the crank before you're back in Healdsburg.

Note: Whether on a bike or in a car, you can be thrown in jail if your blood-alcohol level exceeds 0.8 percent. So how much can you legally taste? It depends on your body size. Some people can have as little as two small drinks and be too drunk to hit the road. For more specific information see the California DUI Web site at www.dui.com.

Vine Country Ramble

GRATON — EAST SIDE ROAD — WINDSOR — CHARLES SCHULZ
MEMORIAL AIRPORT — WILLOWSIDE ROAD — GRATON

N eat trellised vineyards corrugate the plains and hills of Sonoma County, their appearance changing with the season. In winter vine trunks stand dark against the greening grass, made lush by the frequent rain. In spring mustard flowers bloom electric yellow between the rows, soon followed by young shoots springing from the vine wood. In summer a confusion of green leaves overtakes the trellises, hiding clusters of slow-ripening fruit beneath the boughs. And in autumn, with grapes removed and crushed, vine leaves glow yellow, crimson, and purple, before dropping to the ground in a colorful carpet.

Whatever the season, a spin through the vineyards of Sonoma County is always good for the body and spirit. This ramble threads through some of the finer backroads of the area. Along with two other rides in this book, Dry Creek Ramble and Sweetwater Springs Cruise, it is where you will enjoy quintessential wine country landscapes. But unlike the other two routes, there are no wineries to visit on this ramble. So if the wine scene is your bag, look to one of the other rides. But if you want to stay somewhat farther away from the thirsty hordes, while still enjoying the region's bucolic ambiance, then this one's for you. And along with the great scenery, this ramble is about as flat as they come in these parts, with only a few, short climbs to contend with. Traffic is also light, though there are several road crossings where you need to proceed with caution.

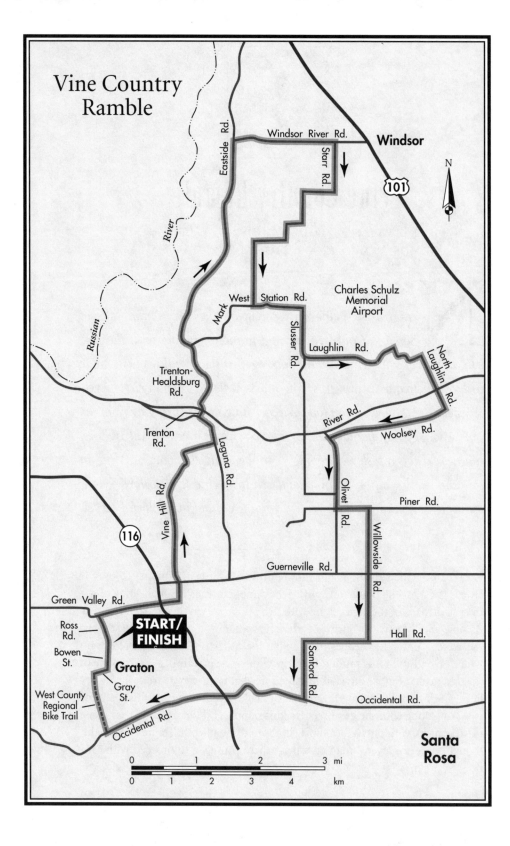

Beginning in the tiny hamlet of Graton, where you can get a great meal at the Willow Wood Market, the ramble heads out of town and across Highway 116, a busy two-lane that connects the towns of Forestville and Sebastopol. Turning left on Vine Hill Road after crossing the highway, you pass along hilltop vineyards with great views of the Mayacamas Mountains to the east. After crossing River Road at mile 4.6 (watch for speeding cars), you head up peaceful Trenton-Healdsburg Road to Eastside Road. Here you descend to the northern reaches of the Russian River valley, which opens into a wide, flat plain stretching all the way to Healdsburg. But you exit the valley before Healdsburg at mile 9.2, heading east toward Windsor, one of the fastest-growing condo towns in the county. If you ride just a little ways beyond the turnoff at Starr Road at mile

THE BASICS

Start: Ross Road and Graton Road in downtown Graton.

Length: 28.6 miles.

Terrain: Generally flat, with a few easy climbs and descents. Narrow roads with minimal shoulders and blind corners—always ride single file.

Food: The Graton Market in Graton is a good place to stock up on snacks. The Willow Wood Market, also in Graton, offers sit-down dining with good healthy fare. A few restaurants are also available just off the route in Windsor.

For more information: Dave's Bike Sport, 353 College Avenue, Santa Rosa, CA 95401; (707) 528-3283.

Maps: DeLorme *Northern California Atlas and Gazetteer,* map 83; Krebs Cycle Products, *North San Francisco Bay and Wine Country* map.

While sampling the bucolic beauty of Starr Road near Windsor, remember to ride single file.

0.0 Head north on Ross Road from downtown Graton.

0.6 Right on Green Valley Road. Short climb ahead.

0.9 Cross intersection with busy Highway 116. Exercise caution.

1.2 Left onto Vine Hll Road.

1.4 Cross intersection with busy Guerneville Road. Exercise caution.

3.2 Begin narrow, winding descent.

4.1 Left onto Laguna Road at stop sign.

4.6 Right onto Trenton Road and cross intersection with busy River Road. Exercise caution. Trenton-Healdsburg Road begins.

5.3 Begin moderate climbing.

5.8 Bear left at Mark West Station Road.

5.9 Right onto Eastside Road (summit). Begin moderate descent.

9.2 Right onto Windsor River Road. Begin short climb.

9.7 Summit.

9.8 Windsor town limit; residential area.

10.4 Right on Starr Road.

13.7 Left at T intersection onto unmarked Mark West Station Road.

14.5 Right onto Slusser Road. Airport on left.

15.2 Bear left onto Laughlin Road, continuing around airport.

16.7 Right onto North Laughlin Road.

18.2 Cross intersection at busy River Road. Exercise caution. Continue straight onto Woolsey Road.

20.1 Left onto Olivet Road.

21.3 Left onto Piner Road.

21.8 Right onto Willowside Road.

23.0 Cross busy Guerneville Road.

23.9 Right onto Hall Road.

24.9 Road bends left at Stammer's Corner, becomes Sanford Road.

25.8 Right on Occidental Road.

26.6 Begin moderate climb.

27.1 Summit. Cross intersection with Highway 116 at traffic light.

28.2 Right onto West County Regional Bike Trail (look for yellow barricade on right).

28.3 Right onto Gray Street and immediate left onto Bowen Street.

28.6 Ride ends at Graton Road in downtown Graton.

10.4, you'll find a few fast-food eateries where you can pull in for a pit stop.

After Windsor the road zigs and zags in a series of 90-degree curves on the way to Mark West Station Road, which takes you to the edge of the sleepy Charles Schulz Memorial Airport, named for the beloved *Peanuts* cartoonist who made Santa Rosa his home. You continue around the southern perimeter of the airport—going past the runway approach—and eventually back out to River Road, which you again should tiptoe across.

From here there's more zigging and zagging on relatively quiet backroads surrounded by vines. At Occidental Road, which you reach at mile 25.8, you'll encounter the most traffic, but it has a wide shoulder, and you're on it for little more than a mile. You'll be turning off Occidental Road onto the West County Regional Bike Trail just after crossing Highway 116. Look for the sign and vehicle barricade across the trail. It's an easy one to miss.

From there it's a quick, cool-down spin back to Graton, where you can kick back and enjoy a well-deserved meal or sip the local product at the wine-tasting room on the corner of Ross and Graton Roads. As they pour you a dram, just think of all those vines out there in the sunshine. Raise your glass, make a toast, and thank the biking gods that you are where you are.

Sweetwater Springs Cruise

ARMSTRONG REDWOODS STATE RESERVE — SWEETWATER
SPRINGS ROAD — HOP KILN WINERY — HACIENDA — KORBEL
CHAMPAGNE CELLARS — RIO NIDO —GUERNEVILLE —
ARMSTRONG REDWOODS STATE RESERVE

Armstrong Redwoods State Reserve lies at the bottom of a narrow, steep canyon on the edge of the undeveloped Austin Creek State Recreation Area in western Sonoma County. The 805-acre reserve is famous for its small but majestic stand of old-growth redwoods, some reaching as high as 300 feet and aged more than a thousand years. No matter what the temperature in nearby Guerneville, count on it being around ten degrees cooler, and considerably darker, beneath the boughs of the park's fairylike trees.

Armstrong is where the Sweetwater Springs Cruise begins. This loop winds through the borderlands of vineyards and redwood forests and along the Russsian River valley. Though it is relatively short in distance, this cruise has one long, steady climb, punctuated by a few steep pitches, and a descent that plunges even more steeply than the climb ascends. We've classified it as a cruise, but because of the climbs, you may think it a borderline challenge.

The ride starts at the parking lot at the entrance to Armstrong Redwoods State Reserve. Before setting out you can take an optional 2-mile warm-up through the park, following the signs to the 1,400-year-old Colonel Armstrong tree, named for the lumberman who saw the errors of his clear-cutting ways. The climbing begins early in the ride on lightly traveled Sweetwater Springs Road. As you rise out of the trees, you'll pass the former site of the Great Eastern Quicksilver Mine, an old mercury mine founded in the late 1800s. The

Warm-up spin in Armstrong Redwoods grove.

Start: Armstrong Redwoods State Reserve, Armstrong Redwoods Road north of Guerneville.

Length: 25.9 miles.

Terrain: Steep climbing and descending for approximately 5 miles on Sweetwater Springs Road. Relatively flat terrain through vineyards, with moderate traffic.

Food: Food for Humans in Guerneville offers a great selection of organic produce, sandwiches, and snacks. Hop Kiln Winery sells cheese and crackers, and Korbel offers light gourmet fare at its snack bar.

For more information: Dave's Bike Sport, 353 College Avenue, Santa Rosa, CA 95401; (707) 528-3283.

Maps: DeLorme *Northern California Atlas and Gazetteer,* map 83; Krebs Cycle Products, *North San Francisco Bay and Wine Country* map.

shafts reach more than 400 feet below the surface and were more than 1,000 feet long. Explosions, fire, and earthquakes took many a miner's life down below. And as the signs around the perimeter fence indicate, the area remains a hazardous place and is strictly off-limits.

Beyond the mine the road continues its winding ascent up the shoulder of Mount Jackson. As you approach the summit, the deep green hills of the Coast Range roll off toward the Pacific. On summer afternoons you may see the first fingers of ocean fog creep over the hills. Through the night the fog will fill the valleys, only to burn off by mid-morning the following day.

The descent down Sweetwater Springs Road is very steep, and the road can be sprinkled with sand and gravel in places, so exercise caution. As you descend, you'll again enter a second-growth fir and redwood grove. In spring Porter Creek runs briskly alongside the road. About halfway down you'll pass a pool in the creek at the mouth of a culvert that passes under the road. On hot days it's a great place to take a dip. There are only a few dwellings on Sweetwater Springs, but that has begun to change as rising land prices have caused a recent spike in residential development.

Sweetwater Springs joins Westside Road near historic Hop Kiln Winery. Originally called Walters Ranch, the three-kiln structure that now houses the winery was built in 1905 by Italian stonemasons. The winery has a bike rack in its parking lot and offers picnic tables set near a small pond. You can also purchase cheese, crackers, and other consumables inside the tasting room. Though it is tempting to partake of a glass or two of the local vintage while at Hop Kiln, we strongly recommend that you bring a bottle home for a taste. The next leg of the ride is more heavily trafficked, and the shoulders are thin and gravelly; in other words, you will need all your wits about you.

Compared with Sweetwater Springs Road, the rest of the ride is flat, with the exception of two short hills on Westside Road. The ride down River Road is a breeze, though the traffic is steady and fast; fortunately, there is a good shoulder. Along the way you'll pass the famed Korbel Champagne Cellars,

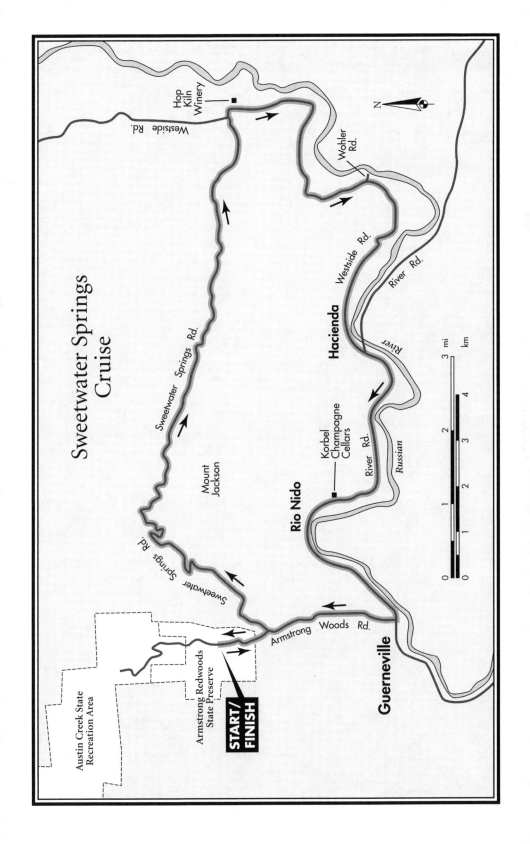

0.0 South on Armstrong Redwoods Road from the parking lot of the state reserve.

0.6 Left onto Sweetwater Springs Road.

1.4 Begin climb.

2.8 False summit. Brief downhill.

4.5 Summit. Begin steep descent.

5.9 Descent levels off.

6.9 Cross over creek (no bridge rails, just culvert pipes), swimming hole immediately below road on left side.

8.4 Begin short climb through oak glades.

9.3 Summit. Begin descent.

11.1 Right onto Westside Road. *Caution:* Narrow two-lane with no shoulder, moderate traffic.

11.2 Hop Kiln Winery.

14.2 Begin short climb.

14.5 Summit. Begin moderate descent.

14.9 Bottom of descent. Intersection with Wohler Road. Continue straight on Westside Road toward Guerneville.

17.4 Begin short climb.

17.8 Summit.

18.1 Right on River Road at Hacienda (merge onto River Road *after* small underpass, not before).

20.6 Pass Korbel Champagne Cellars.

23.3 Right on Armstrong Woods Road at Guerneville.

25.9 Armstrong State Reserve.

which offers tours of its grounds and cellars as well as a small eatery featuring gourmet sandwiches and other delights. Beware of vehicles entering and exiting the Korbel parking lot along River Road.

At Guerneville you return to Armstrong Reserve via a road of the same name. Guerneville is a busy summer resort, particularly on summer weekends when the jazz or blues festival is on. The traffic entering town can sometimes back up for nearly a mile during these times, but if you're careful, you can whiz right by on the shoulder. Before heading back to Armstrong, stop at the Coffee Bazaar on Armstrong Woods Road. It's a favorite local watering hole.

Note: Whether on a bike or in a car, you can be thrown in jail if your blood-alcohol level exceeds 0.8 percent. So how much can you legally taste? It depends on your body size. Some people can have as little as two small drinks and be too drunk to hit the road. For more specific information see the California DUI Web site at www.dui.com.

Russian River Ramble

GUERNEVILLE — MONTE RIO — MOSCOW ROAD — DUNCANS
MILLS —MONTE RIO — MAYS CANYON — GUERNEVILLE

*I*n winter and spring prolonged rain causes the Russian River to occasionally rise in a mad torrent and rush headlong for the ocean, often swamping the towns and roads that line its banks. Some of the older businesses in nearby Guerneville proudly display photos from the more severe floods. In them you'll see buildings up to their eaves in water, with River Road—the town's main thoroughfare—looking more like a river than a road. Obviously, it's best to avoid the Russian when it's angry, unless you have a strong amphibious streak.

But in summer the mighty Russian sleeps low in its bed, and canoes are once again used for recreation rather than basic transportation. Visitors throng to the river area for boating, bicycle racing and touring, concerts, and various gay and lesbian festivals (the region is a haven for San Francisco's gay community). Though the tourist traffic can get heavy at times, there are subtle but effective ways of getting beyond it and into the quiet solitude of redwood groves, sunny vineyards, and wide-open pasture.

This leisurely ramble is best enjoyed during the summer months, not only because it's sunnier then, but because it would otherwise involve crossing the river twice without the aid of a bridge. Each year from early June through September, the Sonoma County Road Department constructs three temporary bridges across the Russian River to offer greater access to the homes and cottages located on the bank opposite River Road. These "summer bridges," as they are called, consist of one lane of packed sand and gravel, bulldozed into place across the idle river. In fall they are ritually scooped out of the riverbed, allowing

Grizzly memories near the information center in Duncans Mills.

the water to resume its natural course. This ramble uses two of these bridges, so be sure they are in place before heading out. Contact the Sonoma County Road Department, Armstrong Woods Road, Guerneville; (707) 869–2024.

Beginning at the Coffee Bazaar in Guerneville, a local watering hole and popular bike rendezvous, you head west through town to River Road and eventually Monte Rio, a "vacation wonderland." After taking the old railroad bridge over the river, you bank right onto Moscow Road, a quiet, shady backroad through the redwoods lined with old cottages and summer homes. This road brings you to Duncans Mills, the former western terminus of the Northwest Pacific Railroad, and the start of the King Ridge Challenge (also in this chapter). There's a grocery store and several restaurants here, and you can often feel cool sea air waft in from the nearby Pacific.

THE BASICS

Start: Coffee Bazaar on Armstrong Woods Road in Guerneville.

Length: 23.7 miles.

Terrain: Flat, with a few short hills. Light traffic on most roads, with heavier traffic along River Road.

Food: Guerneville has a grocery store and numerous restaurants, including Sparks, an all-vegan gourmet eatery. Duncans Mills has a general store, coffee shop, and two restaurants.

For more information: Russian River Bikes, 14070 Mill Street, Guerneville, CA 95446; (707) 869–1455.

Maps: DeLorme *Northern California Atlas and Gazetteer*, maps 83 and 93; Krebs Cycle Products, *North San Francisco Bay and Wine Coutnry* map.

From Duncans Mills you can either retrace your route to Monte Rio via Moscow Road or turn right on River Road, which will also take you back to Monte Rio. The latter option is more heavily traveled, and there is a half-mile narrow, tree-darkened section with no shoulder. Whichever you choose, after returning to Monte Rio, head down River Road to the turnoff for Vacation Beach Road, which takes you across the first "summer bridge." The road across the river is unpaved, narrow, and a little rough (with a corrugated metal grate) but usually firm. You'll pass a leaky timber dam and fish ladder on the left and climb up the other side to Neely Road, another shady cruise through clusters of summer cottages and tall redwoods. You'll pass a turnoff for another summer bridge along the way (don't take it) and come out on Highway 116, which takes you up to Mays Canyon. The canyon provides another peaceful roll through the redwoods and takes you past hilly Porter Bass Vineyards. You again pop out on Highway 116 and coast down to Odd Fellows Park Road, which takes you across your second summer bridge.

From there carefully cross River Road and head west. Along the way you'll pass the Korbel Champagne Cellars, which offers tours and free tastings (just

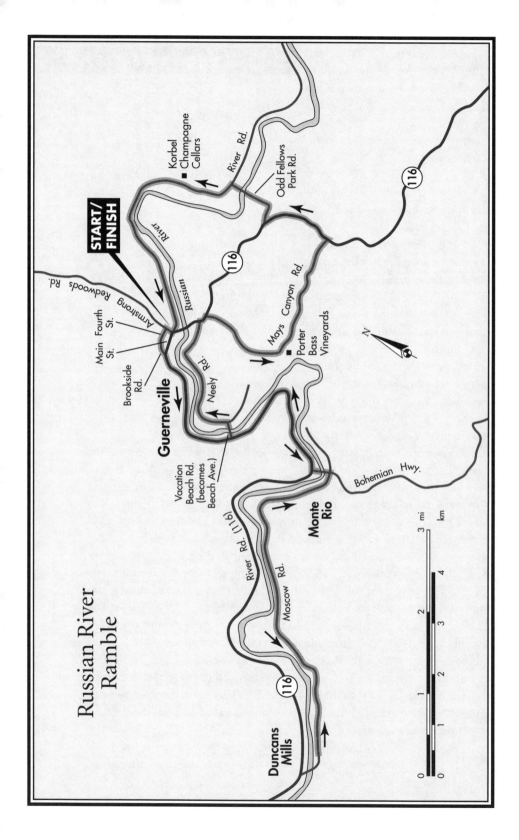

Russian River Ramble

START/FINISH

Korbel Champagne Cellars

River Rd.

Odd Fellows Park Rd.

116

River

Russian River

Armstrong Redwoods Rd.

Main St.
Fourth St.
Brookside Rd.

Guerneville

Mays Canyon Rd.

Porter Bass Vineyards

116

N

Neely Rd.

Vacation Beach Rd. (becomes Beach Ave.)

Bohemian Hwy.

Monte Rio

River Rd. (116)

Moscow Rd.

116

Duncans Mills

3 mi
km

0   1   2   3
0   1   2   3   4

0.0 From the Coffee Bazaar head north for 1 block on Armstrong Woods Road and then turn left on Fourth Street.

0.3 Fourth Street curves left and becomes Brookside Road.

0.4 Right on Main Street, which becomes River Road (County Highway 116).

4.2 Veer left at first stop in Monte Rio and then turn left at second stop onto Bohemian Highway and cross bridge.

4.4 Right onto Main Street after bridge.

4.5 Right onto Moscow Road.

7.5 Cross bridge over Russian River.

7.6 Duncans Mills.

7.7 River Road (Highway 116) intersection. Return on Moscow Road to Monte Rio or turn right on River Road. Beware of half-mile narrows with no shoulder on River Road.

11.6 Veer left, staying on River Road (Highway 116) at Monte Rio.

13.8 Right on Vacation Beach Road. Descend and cross summer bridge.

14.0 Straight on Beach Avenue.

14.1 Left onto Neely Road.

15.4 Veer right to stay on Neely Road.

15.9 Right onto Highway 116.

16.0 Right on Mays Canyon Road.

16.4 Begin gradual climbing.

18.2 Summit at Porter Bass Vineyards.

18.6 Left on Highway 116.

19.5 Right on Odd Fellows Park Road.

20.2 Cross summer bridge.

20.3 Left onto River Road.

20.5 Korbel Champagne Cellars. Beware of vehicles entering and exiting parking lot.

23.7 Ride ends at Armstrong Redwoods Road, Guerneville.

don't let it go to your head). And remember that you parked your car back in Guerneville, another 3 miles down the road. (Beware of cross traffic and opening doors as you approach town.) Head back to cap off the day with some of the most extraordinary vegetarian food on the planet at renowned Sparks Restaurant in downtown Guerneville. And, if you haven't gotten your feet wet yet, cool off with a dip at Johnson's Beach, just off First Street.

6

King Ridge Challenge

DUNCANS MILLS — CAZADERO — GUALALA RIVER —
TIMBERHILL —MEYERS GRADE ROAD — RUSSIAN GULCH
STATE PARK — JENNER —DUNCANS MILLS

*L*ong, hard bicycle rides are as much a journey of the mind as *they are of the body. Writer William Saroyan in his 1952 mem-oir* The Bicycle Rider in Beverly Hills *described the physical action of riding a bike as having a corresponding action in mind, memory, and imagination. Riding was a stimulus, he believed, that permitted one to see the limitless potential in all things.*

Ancient oaks grace the hilltops along King Ridge Road.

The King Ridge Challenge is one of those rides that stirs the imagination as it exercises the body. One climb leads to another, and the descents lend new meaning to the phrase "white knuckle." From the shady redwood forests that grow on the banks of Austin Creek to the summits of the pointed but grassy Coast Range, you are treated to an endless array of inspiring delights. In spring the hills are Irish green, and it doesn't take too great a flight of fancy to believe that you are on the Emerald Isle or perhaps the Scottish highlands. In summer the slopes turn tawny and are often shrouded in fog, suggesting a New Zealand or Tazmanian landscape.

Beginning in Duncans Mills, the former western terminus of the Northwest Pacific Railroad (at present a railroad museum), you head briefly east on Highway 116 (also called River Road) to the Cazadero Highway, a lightly traveled two-lane. At mile 7.4 you enter the woodsy hamlet of Cazadero. You may see other riders having a cool drink on the deck of the town's general store. You may want to join them and perhaps trade road stories as you rehydrate. You won't have another opportunity to fill your tanks until you reach Jenner at mile 45.7.

Just after town you veer right onto King Ridge Road. The first few miles on King Ridge are mild, with the real climbing coming at about mile 10. After that it's up and down and up and down for the rest of the journey. The first very steep descent

THE BASICS

Start: Moscow Road and River Road (California Highway 116) at Duncans Mills. Parking is available along Moscow Road.

Length: 50.8 miles.

Terrain: Long climbs and steep, sharply curved descents on lightly traveled roads. Traffic heaviest on Highways 1 and 116. Beware of RVs there.

Food: Duncans Mills has a general store, coffee shop, and two restaurants. There's also a general store at Cazadero and a restaurant and general store in Jenner. Bring along snacks and plenty of water.

For more information: Dave's Bike Sport, 353 College Avenue, Santa Rosa, CA 95401; (707) 528–3283. www.srcc.com. Santa Rosa Cycling Club; www.srcc.com

Maps: DeLorme *Northern California Atlas and Gazetteer*, maps 82 and 92; Krebs Cycle Products, *California North Coast* map.

begins at mile 24.5 and plummets down to the Gualala River. The climbing resumes immediately after you cross the metal-grate bridge over the river. At mile 27.4 you'll pass the exclusive resort of Timberhill, where movie stars fly in on helicopters and pay more than $1,000 per night to enjoy outrageous luxuries in the coastal outback. (You may encounter some construction vehicles here, as the resort is currently being renovated.)

At mile 35.8 you'll come to Fort Ross Road. If you want to avoid the RV traffic ahead on Highway 1, you can turn left here. Expect 10 miles of mostly downhill to Cazadero on Fort Ross Road (though there are a few climbs thrown in along the way). If you can deal with having to ride on a shoulderless and sometimes trafficky road for about 15 miles, then continue straight to Highway 1 on Meyers Grade Road. Regardless of which you choose, be sure to double-check your brakes here; you are about to put them to the test on grades that sometimes reach 18 percent. The most exhilarating, though not the steepest, section is along Highway 1 just before Russian Gulch State Park. This

0.0 East on Highway 116 from intersection with Moscow Road at Duncans Mills.

1.1 Left onto Cazadero Highway. Begin climbing gradually.

7.4 Cazadero.

7.8 Veer right onto King Ridge Road (not to Fort Ross Sea Ranch).

10.4 Begin climbing more steeply.

11.1 Summit. Begin descent.

11.9 Bottom of descent.

12.1 Begin climbing steeply.

13.4 Summit. Begin steep, short descent. Road follows ridge top.

15.0 Begin steep descent.

15.3 Start slow climb up next ridge.

15.7 Steep switchbacks.

16.0 Summit. Short descent and then follow ridge top.

17.0 Great views along knife-edge ridge.

20.2 Begin climbing.

20.5 Summit.

20.7 Descend steeply.

23.1 Bottom descent. Begin short climb.

24.5 Left onto Hauser Bridge Road toward Plantation. Go down steeply.

25.8 Bottom of gnarly descent at bridge over Gualala River. Begin climbing.

27.4 Timberhill development.

27.7 Summit.

28.3 Left onto Seaview Road toward Jenner.

29.0 Begin climbing.

30.8 Summit.

31.8 Pass Timber Cove Road. Go straight toward Jenner. Begin climbing.

35.3 Left at intersection with Fort Ross Road. Seaview becomes Fort Ross Road here.

35.8 Continue straight on unmarked Meyers Grade Road, where Fort Ross Road veers left. (Ten-mile option to return to Cazadero Highway via Fort Ross Road begins here.)

37.7 Summit. Begin long descent (18 percent at times)

40.8 Left on Highway 1 toward Jenner. Begin long descent. Beware of traffic on winding switchbacks (Dramamine Drive).

42.7 Bottom of descent. Russian Gulch State Park on right.

45.7 Jenner.

47.0 Left onto Highway 116 toward Guerneville.

50.8 End at Moscow Road, Duncans Mills.

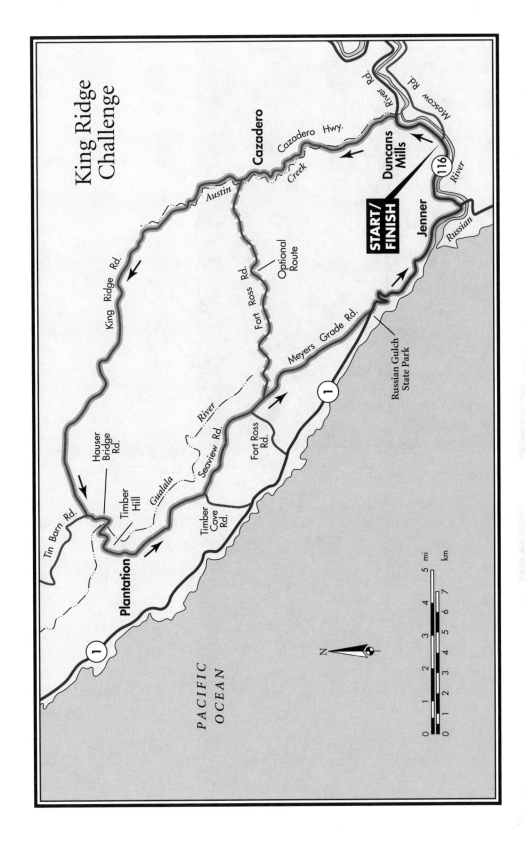

King Ridge Challenge

Cazadero

Duncans Mills

START/FINISH

Jenner

Cazadero Hwy.

Creek

Austin

River Rd.

Moscow Rd.

116

River

Russian

Optional Route

Fort Ross Rd.

King Ridge Rd.

Meyers Grade Rd.

Russian Gulch State Park

1

Hauser Bridge Rd.

Timber Hill

Gualala

River

Seaview Rd.

Fort Ross Rd.

Timber Cove Rd.

Tin Barn Rd.

Plantation

1

PACIFIC OCEAN

N

0   1   2   3   4   5 mi

0   1   2   3   4   5   6   7 km

Can you make the grade on King Ridge Road.?

prolonged descent, locally known as Dramamine Drive, has expansive views of the Pacific and is very, very curvy.

The ocean scenery continues all the way to Jenner. Just before you reach town, stop at one of the pullouts on the right, overlooking the mouth of the Russian River. Here you're likely to see what looks like rows of bleached driftwood logs lying on the sandy banks. Listen and you may hear them barking. No, the sounds are not the aftereffects of Dramamine Drive. What you see is not driftwood but seals basking in the sun.

The last few miles on Highway 116 to Duncans Mills usually come with a tailwind, courtesy of the wide, blue Pacific. As you shift into your big ring and settle into a steady cadence, you'll feel as though you can almost fly. It's a great cap to a difficult but wonderful ride, one that inspires and frees the mind to wander on a host of different roads.

Occidental Cruise

OCCIDENTAL — COLEMAN VALLEY — PACIFIC COAST —
THE RUSSIAN RIVER — POMO VALLEY — OCCIDENTAL

T he town of Occidental is a tiny redwood getaway on the western edge of Sonoma County, between Santa Rosa and the ocean. Founded as a railhead for the lumber industry, Occidental now thrives on retirees, tourists, and its restaurants. Occidental also happens to be one of the most charming towns in California.

The Occidental Cruise is another redwoods-to-the-sea ride, really the best type of ride in this part of the country because of the remarkable contrasts. And like other rides along the coast, it includes its share of long, tough hills (a borderline challenge). Beginning in the lush, ferny, dimly lit world of the Bohemian Highway—the name says it all—the route climbs over the Coast Range and traverses open meadows to reach a stop-you-dead-in-your-tracks view of the Pacific Ocean. From way up high you plummet to the ocean's very edge. Then after 10 miles of windblown but brightly lit seascape on Highway 1, the cruise returns inland, coursing up the wild Pomo Valley on the stair-stepped dirt switchbacks of Willow Creek Road.

The ride begins in downtown Occidental. A good starting place is Howard's Station, a popular local breakfast spot. From there roll down to the four-way stop and make a left on Coleman Valley Road. Watch for blackberries along this stretch of road from mid-summer onward. Also on this stretch is the old Coleman Valley School, one of the oldest schoolhouses in California (1864); you can't miss it. After the initial climb out of Occidental, Coleman becomes rolling and opens into meadows that lead through a series of sheep and cow farms and finally to the abrupt 1,000-foot descent to Highway 1.

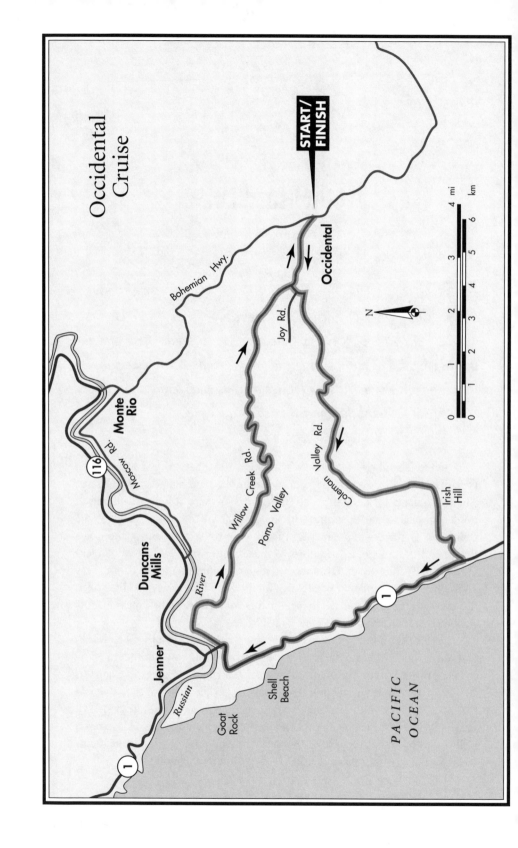

Cyclists should take care on Highway 1 because of tourist traffic, especially on weekends. Interesting side trips include Shell Beach, where there are hiking trails, and Goat Rock State Park.

Willow Creek Road is quite a contrast to Highway 1. The turnoff is right at the corner of the Sizzling Tandor Restaurant. (If you cross the Russian River, you've missed the turn.) The first thing you see when you turn is a sign that says: ROAD CLOSED, NO THROUGH TRAFFIC. But don't worry, these signs are to prevent tourists from getting lost. The road is open but soon turns to dirt and gravel for about 5 miles. There are two steep sections here, but the road is usually quite rideable on a road bike.

A few words of warning: During hunting season (six weeks in late

THE BASICS

Start: Howard's Station, Bohemian Highway, Occidental.

Length: 28.6 miles.

Terrain: Rolling hills, steep descending; two major climbs, one on dirt. The rural roads have no traffic. Highway 1 is fairly busy. Heavy-duty tires are recommended on Willow Creek Road.

Food: In Occidental there are a number of excellent restaurants. On the coast water is available at campgrounds. At the base of Willow Creek, there is an Indian restaurant, The Sizzling Tandoor.

For more information: Dave's Bike Sport, 353 College Avenue, Santa Rosa, CA 95401; (707) 528–3283.

Maps: DeLorme *Northern California Atlas and Gazetteer,* maps 92 and 93; Krebs Cycle Products, *California North Coast* map.

Leaving the Pomo Valley on Willow Creek Road.

0.0 From Howard's Station turn right (north) on Bohemian Highway and left on Coleman Valley Road. Begin climbing.

1.7 Bear left at the intersection of Willow Creek Road. Stay on Coleman Valley.

1.8 Summit.

1.9 Bear right at the intersection of Joy Road. Stay on Coleman Valley.

10.0 Right on Highway 1. Watch for traffic on weekends.

16.4 Right on Willow Creek Road, which turns to dirt in approximately 2 miles. Continue on through major climbing. (An alternate paved route would be to go to Highway 116 just over the Russian River and turn right, right again on Moscow Road in Duncans Mills, and right on Bohemian Highway in Monte Rio to Occidental. The climb up Bohemian Highway is long and can get trafficky at times.)

26.9 Left on Coleman Valley. Down the hill to Occidental.

28.4 Right on Bohemian Highway.

28.6 Ride ends at Howard's Station.

August and September) and during "mud season" (usually November through April), Willow Creek Road probably should be avoided. Also, some of this road is open range, and there are occasionally cows on the road. Those riding mountain bikes should note that although there are tempting trails off Willow Creek, they are not legal.

The cruise ends with a roller-coaster, paved section on Willow Creek and then a rush back down Coleman Valley Road to Occidental.

West Bay Area

Cheese Factory Cruise

MARIN FRENCH CHEESE COMPANY — MARSHALL — POINT REYES
STATION — MARIN FRENCH CHEESE COMPANY

I*f you're a Wallace and Gromit movie fan, you know the lengths some people will go for fine cheese. The Marin French Cheese Company facility has indeed lured many a Bay Area cyclist to its tasting room for their own* Grand Day Out. *You are sure to run into a few of them relaxing on the factory's picnic grounds, after a hearty round of sampling.*

Proper etiquette dictates that you do eventually buy something, but don't feel shy about nibbling the goods. Even in your sweaty, dirty bike clothes, sporting your freshly plastered helmet-head, you won't be shunned—this is biking territory, and the folks are used to our kind here.

The site of a working ranch and cheese-making facility for five generations, the cheese factory is located in the heart of cow country on Point Reyes/Petaluma Road between Nicasio and Petaluma. The factory serves as the ride start and finish, and it is one of the few signs of civilization on the loop—unless you consider cows civilized. Once you leave the Camembert behind and give your cranks a spin, you'll roll into a different world.

The first 10 miles provide fast and easy riding on intensely rural roads. It's almost impossible to believe that you're only 40 miles away from the urban sprawl of San Francisco and its surrounding areas. After 10 miles you reach what's known as the Marshall Wall. This 2-mile climb is an unrelenting pull with at least two false summits before you reach the top. Still, the name is more intimidating than the actual climb. And once you reach the summit, the views of Point Reyes and Tomales Bay are absolutely euphoric. Then again, maybe it's just those endorphins that are coursing through your body.

The backside of the Marshall Wall is much steeper and will leave you thankful that you do not to have to return this way. Down in the tiny town of Marshall, you'll find rickety oyster bars and a few random stores perched on the edge of Tomales Bay. Following the Shoreline Highway, you'll get a roller-coaster ride of whoop-dee-do hills that's often made easier by benevolent tailwinds. After nearly 7 miles of this fun, you'll experience a few longer

Fleurs-de-lis mark the entrance to the Cheese Factory.

climbs before dropping down into the tiny, but hip, burg of Point Reyes Station (situated on a short spur off the loop).

THE BASICS

Start: Marin French Cheese Company, Point Reyes/Petaluma Road. Take Highway 101 to downtown Novato. From there take Novato Boulevard east until it intersects with Point Reyes/Petaluma Road.

Length: 34.6 miles.

Terrain: Two major climbs; lots of rolling hills. Moderate traffic on Point Reyes/Petaluma Road. Heavier traffic on Highway 1.

Food: The cheese company has—you guessed it—lots of cheese and cheese-related snacks, as well as chips, sodas, and delicious fruit. If you like raw oysters, stop in Marshall at one of the bayside oyster bars. Otherwise, you can stock up on snacks in Point Reyes Station, where there are several cafes and a great grocery store situated right on the main road.

For more information: Petaluma Visitors Program, 799 Baywood Drive, Suite 1, Petaluma, CA 94954; (707) 762–2785. Bicycle Factory, 1111 Grant Avenue, Novato, CA 94930; (415) 892–5538.

Maps: DeLorme *Northern California Atlas and Gazetteer*, map 93; Krebs Cycle Products, *California North Coast* map.

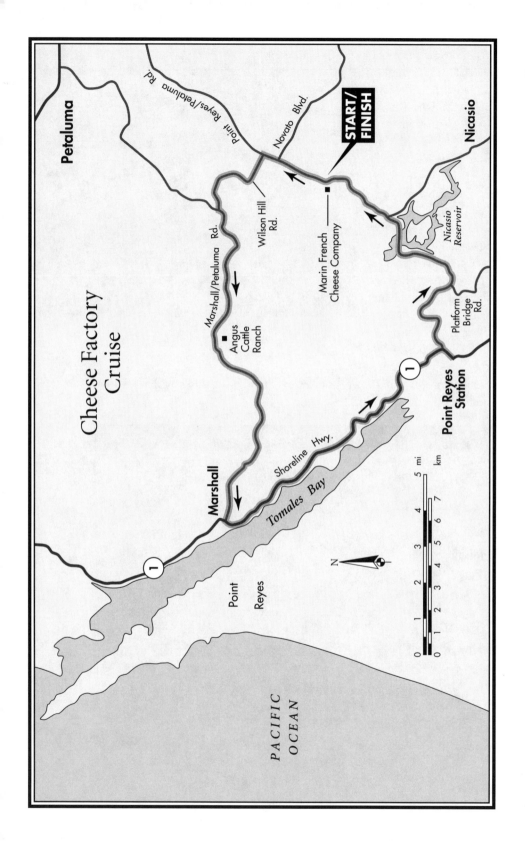

Cheese Factory Cruise

0.0 From the cheese factory turn left onto Point Reyes/Petaluma Road.

0.9 Left onto Hicks Valley (Wilson Hill Road) toward Marshall.

3.7 Left on Marshall/Petaluma Road.

10.0 Aberdeen Angus Cattle Ranch. Begin climb up Marshall Wall!

12.0 Summit.

14.6 Marshall. Left onto Shoreline Highway (Highway 1).

24.7 Veer right, staying on Highway 1 into Point Reyes Station.

25.0 Point Reyes Station. Turnaround point. After sightseeing ride back up the hill on Highway 1.

25.3 Right onto Point Reyes/Petaluma Road.

28.4 Left at **T** intersection onto Platform Bridge Road.

28.9 Nicasio Reservoir.

31.1 Begin climb.

32.6 Summit.

34.6 Ride ends at Marin French Cheese Company.

You get even more sweet cows and rural scenery on the way back, though the traffic is heaviest on this leg. And, of course, as fate would have it, there's another major climb less than 4 miles from the end of the ride. This final push begins just past the Nicasio Reservoir and heads upward on a fairly busy road back to the cheese factory, where you can again chill out and mooch free samples of cheese.

9

Bolinas Challenge

BOLINAS — STINSON BEACH — MUIR WOODS NATIONAL
MONUMENT — MOUNT TAMALPAIS STATE PARK — BOLINAS

O*ne of the more famous mountains in the annals of bicycling
history is Marin County's Mount Tamalpais. Cyclists owe
much to her steep, furrowed flanks, as the sport of mountain biking was
born there. In the 1970s the Canyon Gang, an informal group of gonzo
adventurers, held races down Mount Tam's fire roads on balloon-tire
bikes equipped with coaster brakes. Word quickly spread, and before long
a bevy of two-wheeled inventors were bent on improving the perform-
ance of the crude, clunky machines. The rest, of course, is fat-tire history.*

The grade out of Stinson Beach.

Mount Tam and environs
remain a testament to cycling
fun. Though much of the
reverie still focuses on the dirt
aspects, there's much to
yahoo about on the paved
routes as well.

The Bolinas Challenge
follows some of the more
spectacular roads along Marin
County's coastline and up
the spine of its most prominent peak. The ride begins in
the tiny coastal hamlet of

Bolinas, a haven for poets and artists that has remained off the tourist track thanks, in part, to the locals' former, and now famous, habit of stealing the town's Highway 1 turnoff sign.

The ride heads south on Highway 1 along the Bolinas Lagoon to Stinson Beach, a popular weekend sunbathing hangout. Here the first significant, but relatively gentle, climb snakes up the rocky coast. Thereafter, the views are spectacular, particularly on sunny afternoons when the fog has receded and the ocean is pure lapis lazuli.

But you are hardly alone out on this stretch of road, particularly on weekends, which attracts an assortment of vehicles both wide, as in motor home, and thin, as in motorcycle. Of course, this is to be expected given the proximity to San Francisco. But what is not expected is the polite distance most drivers offer cyclists. The reason, I believe, is due to a series of signs posted along the highway, imploring drivers to SHARE THE ROAD. A marked drop in driver manners occurs farther along on the Panoramic Highway, a narrow two-lane where heady Marinites tend to drive their Jags and Porsches much too fast for their own, and others', good. More signs are needed.

But before that there's plenty of ascending and descending along the coast, as the road navigates the drainages that have scooped out the coastal ridge. After one last prolonged climb, the road veers east at mile 12 and plunges downward, reaching near sea level at Muir Woods Road. This flat, quiet byway leads up to the gates of the 560-acre Muir Woods National Monument, named for the renowned philosopher and naturalist, John Muir. Though it can be busy at peak vacation times, the monument's grove is worthy of a stop, with 6 miles of trails that take you through the Bay Area's last stand of old-growth redwood.

After the monument Muir Woods Road starts its long climb to the Panoramic Highway. Though there are a few, brief downhill respites, the route

THE BASICS

Start: Bolinas. Take the Highway 1 exit off Highway 101 and follow it past Stinson Beach to Bolinas. Parking is limited in town, so consider parking outside of town on Olema/Bolinas Road.

Length: 34.2 miles.

Terrain: Three extended climbs, with many smaller climbs and rollers in between. Traffic varies according to the time of day and week but is generally very light on all but the Panoramic Highway and Highway 1.

Food: Either the grocery store in Bolinas or Stinson Beach, the only stores along the route, are good for stocking up. The Coast Café in Bolinas offers excellent seafood and other fare.

For more information: The Bicycle Trail Coalition of Marin and Marin Trails offers bike-riding tips to the area. See www.btcmarin.org and www.marintrails.com or Marin Valley Cyclery, 369 Miller Avenue, Mill Valley, CA 94941; (415) 388–6774.

Maps: DeLorme *Northern California Atlas and Gazetteer*, maps 103 and 104; Krebs Cycle Products, *California North Coast* map.

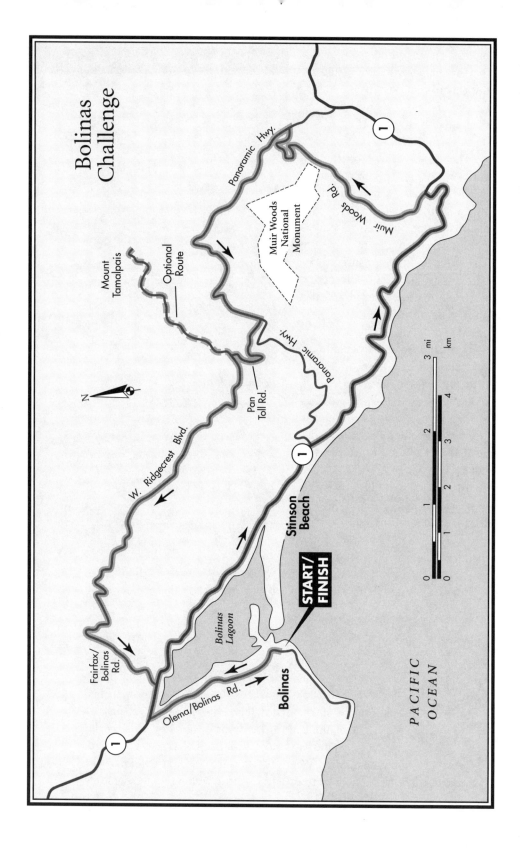

0.0 From Bolinas head north on Olema/Bolinas Road.

0.9 Right at stop sign to continue on Olema/Bolinas Road.

2.1 Right on unmarked road toward Highway 1.

2.2 Right on Highway 1.

6.5 Stinson Beach.

6.8 Begin climbing along coast.

8.2 Summit.

8.6 Begin winding descent.

9.5 Bottom descent. Begin rolling hills through coastal drainages.

11.0 Begin longer climb.

11.6 Summit.

12.0 Begin steep, winding prolonged descent.

13.2 Left onto Muir Woods Road. *Caution:* Blind intersection.

15.8 Entrance to Muir Woods National Monument on left. Begin climbing.

17.0 Hard left (and up) on Panoramic Highway toward Mount Tamalpias.

18.3 Summit. Begin rolling hills.

20.6 Begin climbing.

22.0 Right onto Pan Toll Road toward Mount Tamalpias and West Ridgecrest Boulevard.

23.6 Left onto West Ridgecrest Boulevard (right for optional out-and-back 5.4-mile spur to summit of Mount Tam). Summit. Begin rolling hills.

27.6 Left onto Fairfax/Bolinas Road. Begin long, winding descent.

32.0 Continue straight at stop sign at Highway 1 intersection.

32.1 Left onto Olema/Bolinas Road.

33.3 Left at stop sign to continue on Olema/Bolinas Road.

34.2 End at Bolinas.

continues to climb up and up in the shadow of Mount Tam. Finally, it summits at the turnoff for West Ridgecrest Boulevard, an absolutely glorious, quiet park road that offers orgasmic views of Stinson Beach and the Bolinas peninsula. Energetic riders may want to do the extra 5.4-mile up and back to the summit of Mount Tam before proceeding down Ridgecrest.

Bolinas/Fairfax Road is 6 miles of giggling descent down to Highway 1, where it's just a short but scenic hop back to town. As you roll on into Bolinas, glance up at the high tawny ridge on the left. Yes, you were way up there just moments ago.

Golden Gate Ramble

BLACKIE'S PASTURE PARK — TIBURON — SAN FRANCISCO BAY
FERRY — FISHERMAN'S WHARF — FORT MASON — GOLDEN
GATE BRIDGE — SAUSALITO — BLACKIE'S PASTURE PARK

F ew places have the ability to evoke open-mouthed expressions of wonder like the mile-wide strait that lies between Marin County and San Francisco, otherwise known as the Golden Gate. A tableau of sparkling ocean, crashing waves, and surging currents flanked by luminous green hills, the gate is one of California's most extraordinary features. And the brightly-painted, fog-enshrouded bridge that stretches over the water needs no embellishment, except to say that no journey to San Francisco is complete without a trip across this cabled colonnade.

There are many points from which to take in the beauty of the Golden Gate. This ramble covers most of them. From the Tiburon peninsula you catch the ferry across the bay to Fisherman's Wharf in San Francisco. From there the ride continues around the bay, coursing through the parkland around Fort Mason, where a million good-byes were said during World War II. The ride then follows along the reclaimed marshland known as Crissy Field, spans the Golden Gate Bridge, and threads through the busy bayside hamlet of Sausalito before returning to Tiburon.

Begin at Blackie's Pasture Park on Tiburon Boulevard (just a few miles before downtown Tiburon). The route follows the popular peninsula bike trail, which on weekends you will share with throngs of joggers, walkers, and in-line

Bikes rule on the Golden Gate bridge.

skaters. Tiburon's name derives from the Spanish *punta de tiburon*, which means "shark point." The name still rings true, as the area is the domain of both the wealthy and the extremely wealthy. On any given weekday morning, slick-suited businesspeople board the ferry from the Tiburon dock for San Francisco's financial district and return in the evening gorged from a day of

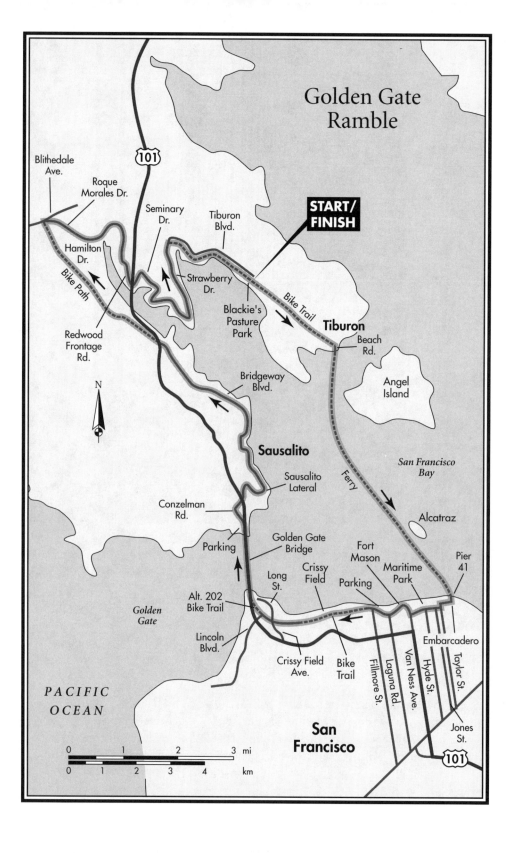

hunting. But there's always a score of cyclists on the ferry, too, whom you can band with should you feel alone.

The ferry ride to San Francisco takes approximately thirty-five minutes and, at last count, was $6.75 one-way (bicycles ride free; see sidebar information for schedule). The boat ride is spectacular and passes by Alcatraz and Angel Island, with lovely views of the Golden Gate. At Pier 41 in busy Fisherman's Wharf—where the ferry arrives—you might experience sensory overload, and you may want to consider simply walking the first mile to Maritime Park. There will be plenty to taste, smell, and see along the way.

Once in Maritime Park, you'll be on a bike trail that takes you all the way to the Golden Gate Bridge. The bridge's west path is reserved for cyclists, and the bike traffic can get surprisingly heavy, though not as heavy as the motorized traffic on the road. You should exercise caution, particularly when negotiating the tight turns around the towers. Also, the bridge is generally always subject to a heavy, and cool, crosswind, which adds to the fun and excitement, assuming you're prepared for it.

Once you've crossed the bridge, the ride is mostly downhill to Sausalito. On weekends the town is a favorite destination, and you will be sharing the road with vehicles packed with gawking tourists, so be on your guard as you approach and enter town. Follow Bridgeway all the way through Sausalito to the bike path that begins at the intersection with Gate 6 Road at mile 12.8, which takes you through the Bothin Marsh Open Space Preserve. Here you get a reprieve from the hustle of town; it's just you, your bike, and the path—oh yes, and a bunch of joggers, walkers, and kids on in-line skates.

After leaving the path you roll through a residential area, slip under the highway, and take Seminary Drive onto the Tiburon peninsula. You'll get

0.0 East on bike trail leaving Blackie's Pasture Park.

2.0 Intersection Beach Road. Continue straight.

2.2 Enter Tiburon. Continue to end of downtown. Ferry terminal behind Boudin Bakery and Café.

2.3 Arrive Pier 41. West on Embarcadero (looks like parking lot) from terminal.

2.5 Left onto Taylor Street (at Fisherman's Grotto) and then right onto Jefferson Street. *Caution:* Streetcar traffic.

2.8 Intersection Jones Street. Continue straight.

3.0 Intersection with Hyde Street. Continue straight to San Francisco Maritime Park and follow bike trail around cove.

3.3 Right on Van Ness Avenue (unmarked). Bike trail ends.

3.4 Left into Fort Mason Park. Follow bike trail up steep hill.

3.6 Summit. Descend into park on a red-paved bike trail.

3.8 Sharp right where trail meets Laguna Road into marina parking lot. Follow parking lot to where two-way bike trail begins parallel to Marina Boulevard at Fillmore Street.

5.9 Left onto Long Street, unmarked (do not go right toward West Bluff picnic area) and immediate right onto Crissy Field Avenue. Begin climbing.

6.1 Summit.

6.2 Bear left onto Lincoln Boulevard (do not go toward Fort Point).

6.3 Right onto Alternate 202 bike trail (a barricade is across the path, closing it to motor vehicles). Follow it to Golden Gate Bridge west path.

6.8 Enter Golden Gate Bridge.

8.4 Enter parking lot at north end of bridge. Follow road up short hill to intersection with Conzelman Road (unmarked) and make right. Short, steep descent ahead.

8.5 Left at stop sign at bottom of hill. *Caution:* Traffic entering/exiting U.S. 101. Road curves underneath 101; beware narrow shoulder in tunnel. Begin long descent on Sausalito-Lateral, which becomes Alexander East Road.

9.8 Enter Sausalito. Alexander East Road becomes Bridgeway. *Caution:* Heavy traffic for 3 miles through downtown.

12.8 Left at intersection with Gate 6 Road onto bike path. Take path through marsh.

15.2 Right on Blithedale Avenue and another right onto Roque Morales Drive.

15.5 Right onto Hamilton Drive.

16.2 Right onto Redwood Frontage Road before Highway 101. Road curves underneath Highway 101 onto east side.

17.0 Right onto Seminary Drive.

17.1 Right at stop sign to continue on Seminary Drive. Follow along shoreline with views of San Francisco to south.

18.1 Begin short climb.

18.3 Summit. Residential area begins at intersection of Chapel Drive.

18.4 Bear left at intersection with Great Circle Drive.

18.5 Continue straight onto Strawberry Drive.

19.7 Right onto bike trail at intersection with Tiburon Boulevard.

20.7 Ride ends at Blackie's Pasture Park.

stunning views of the city across the bay and amble through some quiet residential areas. At mile 19.7 you're back on the bike trail to Blackie's Pasture. You may feel exhausted, windblown, a little shaky from all the traffic, but happy nonetheless for all that came with it.

Daring riders spin through busy Fisherman's Wharf.

San Francisco Ramble

FORT MASON — CRISSY FIELD — OCEAN BEACH —
GOLDEN GATE PARK — PRESIDIO — FORT MASON

*O*nly a few years ago San Francisco made national headlines for its Critical Mass event, a grass-roots ride that involved thousands of cyclists taking to city streets during Friday rush hour. The enormous turnout during the summer of 1997 for this monthly event, which generally attracts only a few handfuls of riders, was spurred by the promise of Mayor Willie Brown to put an end to the protest—Brown was angered by the traffic snarls that ensued during the event. But the bikers that came that fateful summer were not only responding to Mayor Brown's threat, they also wanted safer, more bike-friendly streets.

Thanks to Critical Mass and the efforts of the San Francisco Bike Coalition, which continues to lobby hard for new bicycle routes, the city is more bike-friendly today than it was back then. So as you ride the lanes and dedicated off-street bike paths, think of all those cyclists who bravely pedaled headlong into rush-hour traffic, battling police and commuters for their right to ride, the right that is now yours to enjoy.

Politics aside, this ramble takes you past ocean and bay, along eucalyptus-lined lanes and in and out of neighborhoods. Because this is San Francisco, expect traffic and hills. Though none of the hills are very long, a few can be steep. You should also keep your speed under control on the descents. *A brief word about the bike-route numbering system:* Even-numbered routes indicate an east–west route, odd-numbered routes indicate a north–south route, and three-digit routes indicate a connector route.

Beginning in the Fort Mason area, not far from Greens, the renowned vegetarian restaurant known for its great cookbooks, you head west beside Crissy Field, a restored marsh, on the very well-traveled Bike Lane 2. San Francisco Bay is just a Frisbee's throw away, assuming you do not throw into the wind, which can be fierce at times.

After pedaling past the famed Golden Gate, you'll climb through the forested Golden Gate National Recreation Area on Lincoln Boulevard. You then go on to Sea Cliff, one of the more exclusive areas of the city. After cresting the summit at the Palace of the Legion of Honor (an art museum), you'll get great views of the ocean (to the west) and of green hills encrusted in white stucco homes (to the east).

The ride then follows Ocean

THE BASICS

Start: Fort Mason parking lot at the end of Laguna Street.

Length: 20.3 miles.

Terrain: Several moderate-to-steep (but short) climbs and steep descents. Heavy traffic on streets; bike lanes for part of the route.

Food: Groceries and restaurants are everywhere.

For more information: San Francisco Convention and Visitors' Bureau, 201 Third Street, Suite 900, San Francisco, CA 94103; (415) 391–2000. San Francisco Bike Coalition, 1095 Market Street, #215, San Francisco, CA 94103; (415) 431–2453; www.sfbike.org.

Maps: DeLorme *Northern California Atlas and Gazetteer,* map 104; San Francisco Bike Coalition map.

Cruising the bike lanes along San Francisco Bay.

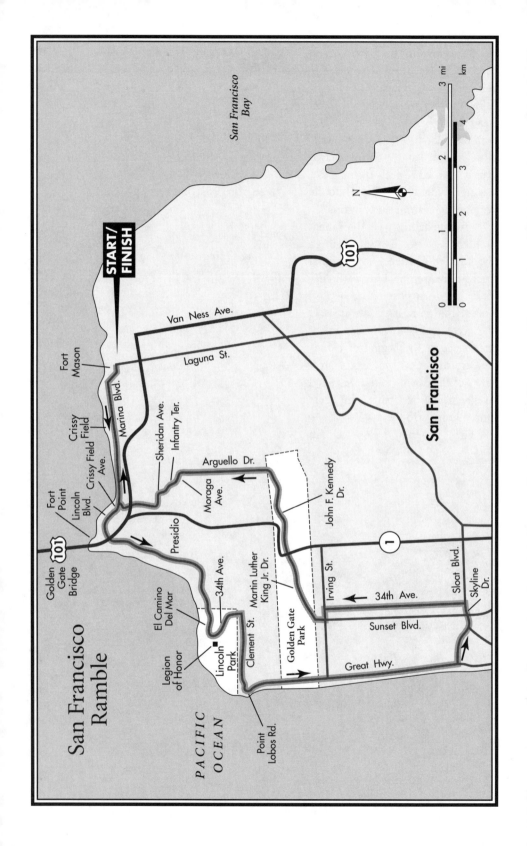

San Francisco Ramble

START/FINISH

San Francisco

San Francisco Bay

PACIFIC OCEAN

Golden Gate Bridge

Fort Point

Lincoln Blvd.

Crissy Field Ave.

Crissy Field

Fort Mason

Marina Blvd.

Sheridan Ave.

Infantry Ter.

Van Ness Ave.

Laguna St.

Presidio

Arguello Dr.

Moraga Ave.

John F. Kennedy Dr.

Martin Luther King Jr. Dr.

Golden Gate Park

El Camino Del Mar

34th Ave.

Legion of Honor

Lincoln Park

Clement St.

Point Lobos Rd.

Irving St.

34th Ave.

Sunset Blvd.

Great Hwy.

Sloat Blvd.

Skyline Dr.

N

101

101

1

0.0 Head west through parking lot, paralleling Marina Boulevard. Pick up bike lane at far end where Fillmore Street intersects Marina Boulevard.

2.1 Left onto Long Street, unmarked (do not go right toward West Bluff picnic area) and immediately right onto Crissy Field Avenue. Begin climb,

2.4 Summit.

2.7 Bear left onto Lincoln Boulevard (do not go toward Fort Point). Begin climbing.

3.0 Summit. Begin descent.

4.0 Bottom of hill. Enter Sea Cliff Development.

4.7 Left onto El Camino del Mar. Begin moderate climb.

5.1 Summit. Left onto Thirty-fourth Street. California Palace of the Legion of Honor on right. Begin steep descent.

5.9 Right onto Clement Street (becomes Seal Rock Road). Begin moderate climb.

6.2 Summit. Descend through residential area.

6.8 Left onto El Camino del Mar.

6.9 Right onto Point Lobos Road. Begin decsent past Cliff House, etc.

7.3 Bottom of descent. Continue straight along Ocean Beach following Great Highway (off-street bike path runs along east side of road from Fulton Street to Sloat Drive).

10.1 Left onto Sloat Drive (following Bike Route 50).

10.8 Merge onto Skyline Drive.

11.0 Left onto Thirty-fourth Avenue (following Bike Route 85).

13.1 Left onto Irving Street, ride 2 blocks and then right onto Sunset Boulevard into Golden Gate Park following Bike Route 85.

13.2 Right onto Martin Luther King Jr. Drive.

14.8 Left following sign toward John F. Kennedy Drive.

15.1 Right onto John F. Kennedy Drive.

15.4 Left at stop sign onto Arguello Drive.

15.6 Bear left at oncoming one-way street. Descend out of park.

15.7 Leave park and continue on Bike Route 65.

16.7 Very steep, but short, hill.

16.8 Enter Presidio Park; bear right following bike route.

17.5 Left onto Moraga Avenue.

17.6 Right onto Infantry Terrace.

17.7 Left onto Sheridan Avenue.

18.0 Right onto Crissy Field Avenue. Descend steeply, going beneath Highway 101.

18.3 Right onto Bike Route 2.

20.3 Fort Mason parking lot.

Distinctive bike-route signs in San Francisco.

Beach and passes the historic Cliff House, which has been serving seafood since 1863. The road's shoulder can get drifted with sand at times, so exercise extra caution if you're on your skinny-tire bike. An off-street bike path runs along the east side of the road from Fulton Street to Sloat Drive, where you also turn inland following Bike Lane 50. From there you then pick up Thirty-fourth Street, taking it through the rolling residential hills of the Sunset District, before reaching Golden Gate Park. The park is one of the best places to be on the weekends, as a number of its roads are closed to vehicles Saturdays and Sundays.

After traversing the park you'll cut across the Richmond District on Arguello, which takes you into the Presidio, a former military base-cum-park. The climb up to the Presidio has a last steep pitch. After winding through the park, a steep downhill ride takes you back to the Crissy Field bike lane, where you retrace part of the first leg of the trip back to Fort Mason.

Crystal Springs Reservoir Cruise

WOODSIDE — CAÑADA ROAD — UPPER CRYSTAL SPRINGS RESERVOIR —
SKYLINE BOULEVARD — KINGS MOUNTAIN ROAD — WOODSIDE

About 15 miles south of San Francisco is a 23,000-acre tract of open space that is largely off-limits to visitors. This is the Crystal Springs Watershed—also known as the San Francisco State Fish and Game Refuge—which the regional water department guards about as closely as the feds guard Fort Knox. Much of the water that collects in the reservoirs at the heart of the property does not originate locally but comes from the Hetch Hetchy Reservoir in Yosemite, more than 150 miles to the east. The water has been flowing from Yosemite into these reservoirs since the 1920s, and it is exceptionally pure, requiring virtually no treatment.

This cruise loops around the southern end of the watershed, beginning in the tiny but upscale village of Woodside. Leaving from the very center of town at Roberts Market, the route follows the relatively straight and flat Cañada Road north. The road, which feels amazingly remote, has an excellent shoulder and is lightly traveled. On Sundays bicyclists, in-line skaters, and self-propelled enthusiasts of every stripe take over a 4-mile stretch of Cañada Road—from Edgewood Road to Highway 92—when San Mateo County closes it off to motorized traffic. On this stretch you'll pass the Filoli Estate National Historic Site, a 654-acre estate that features a forty-five-room mansion designed in 1915 by architect Willis Polk. The mansion appeared in the Warren Beatty movie *Heaven Can Wait* (in which Beatty's character leaves this world via a bike

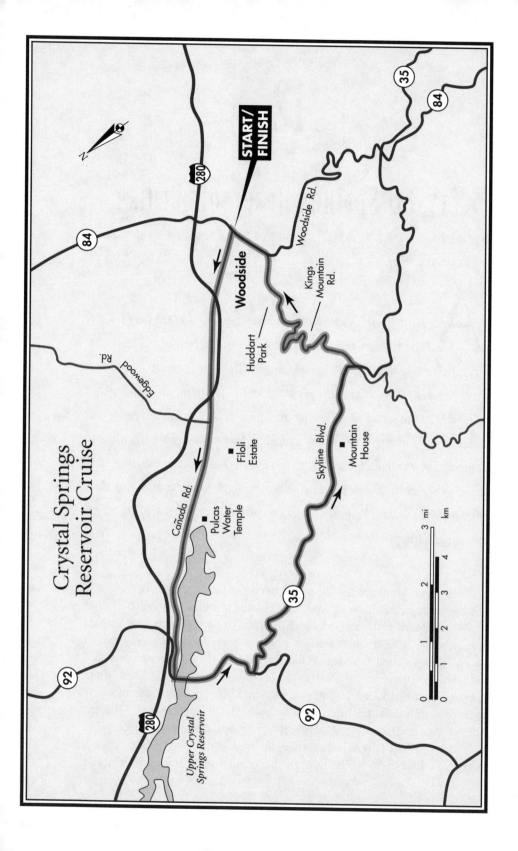

Crystal Springs Reservoir Cruise

START/FINISH

280

84

35

84

Woodside Rd.

Woodside

Kings Mountain Rd.

Huddart Park

Edgewood Rd.

Filoli Estate

Skyline Blvd.

Mountain House

Cañada Rd.

Pulgas Water Temple

35

92

280

92

Upper Crystal Springs Reservoir

N

3 mi
km

wreck) and was the Denver home of the Carringtons in the TV series *Dynasty*.

Beyond Filoli is the Pulgas Water Temple, a Romanesque ring of columns surrounded by lawns and cypress trees. The temple marks the outlet for the aqueduct from Yosemite, which flows into Upper Crystal Springs Reservoir.

Leaving Cañada Road for Highway 92, the route begins a long, ladderlike climb up the Santa Cruz Mountains to Skyline Boulevard. Though it may be sunny when you leave Woodside, you may feel as though you're on the deck of the *Andrea Gail* before she went down by the time you reach Skyline. The wind and fog often conspire on the ridge, reducing visibility and sapping you of all warmth. But if the weather is fair, you'll get views of the ocean and valley that are worth every drop of sweat on the way up.

THE BASICS

Start: Robert's Market, Cañada Road and Woodside Road.

Length: 22.3 miles.

Terrain: One extended climb, generally light traffic, with moderate traffic on Highway 92 and Skyline Boulevard.

Food: Robert's Market in Woodside for groceries. Buck's Restaurant and the Woodside Bakery and Café in Woodside.

For more information: Western Wheelers Bicycle Club, P.O. Box 518, Palo Alto, CA 94302; www.westernwheelers.org. Wheelsmith Bike Shop, 201 Hamilton Avenue, Palo Alto, CA 94301; (650) 324–1919.

Maps: DeLorme *Northern California Atlas and Gazetteer*, maps 104 and 114; Krebs Cycle Products, *South San Francisco Bay and Monterey Bay Areas* map.

Heralding auto-free Sundays on Cañada Road.

0.0 North on Cañada Road from Roberts Market, Woodside.

1.2 Begin downhill and cross under Highway 280.

2.8 Cross again under Highway 280 (continue downhill).

3.4 Pass Edgewood Road.

5.2 Begin climbing. Pass reservoir on left.

5.8 Summit.

6.2 Begin climbing.

6.7 Summit.

7.2 Left onto Highway 92.

7.6 Highway 280 merges in from right (caution!). Stay on 92 west toward Half Moon Bay.

8.1 Begin climbing (narrow shoulder).

9.9 Left onto Skyline Boulevard toward Big Basin.

14.4 Summit.

15.4 Mountain House.

16.6 Left onto Kings Mountain Road.

19.4 Huddart Park.

19.7 Left onto Entrance Way.

21.6 Left onto Woodside Road.

22.3 End at Woodside.

(Traffic, particularly on weekends, can be heavy on Skyline, and there are many blind corners and no shoulder. So beware, or heaven won't wait!)

The payoff for all the climbing comes at mile 14. From there gravity takes over, and, except for heavy braking and banking on the corners, an effortless roll takes you back to Woodside via Kings Mountain Road. This amazing sliver of asphalt includes dozens of hairpin turns that spiral downward to the valley. The descent is tricky, so be sure to exercise caution. On your way down don't miss Huddart Park, one of the peninsula's best-kept secrets (until now). Take a quick look around and make a mental note to come back for a day hike and picnic.

Back on level ground you'll cruise past horse farms, encountering not only four-legged beasts but also those of the four-wheeled variety. Yep, you're back to civilization, with all its grotesque (and glorious) trappings. Stop in at the well-to-do Woodside Market for a final pit stop, where you can mingle with the beautiful people.

Palo Alto Cruise

PALO ALTO — PORTOLA VALLEY — ARASTRADERO BIOLOGICAL
PRESERVE — STANFORD UNIVERSITY — PALO ALTO

P*alo Alto, home to the brainy kids of Stanford University, the silicon chip, and the dot-com boom. This idyllic setting is also a full-on cycling mecca, and the many bike lanes that weave in and out of town are rife with computer geeks, execs, and university profs on their way to work or unwinding after a long day.*

From Palo Alto the ride takes you out of town and lofts you onto the fringe of the surrounding Santa Cruz Mountains. Once there, you'll roll up and down

THE BASICS

Start: Palo Alto Square Shopping Center, corner of El Camino Real and Page Mill Expressway.

Length: 15.6 miles.

Terrain: Mostly rolling hills, with a few moderate climbs and descents. Moderate to light traffic in hills, heavier traffic in Palo Alto.

Food: Myriad restaurants in Palo Alto.

For more information: Western Wheelers Bicycle Club, P.O. Box 518, Palo Alto, CA 94302; www.westernwheelers.org. Wheelsmith Bike Shop, 201 Hamilton Avenue, Palo Alto, CA 94301; (650) 324–1919.

Maps: DeLorme Northern *California Atlas and Gazetteer*, maps 114 and 115; Krebs Cycle Products, *South San Francisco Bay and Monterey Bay Areas* maps.

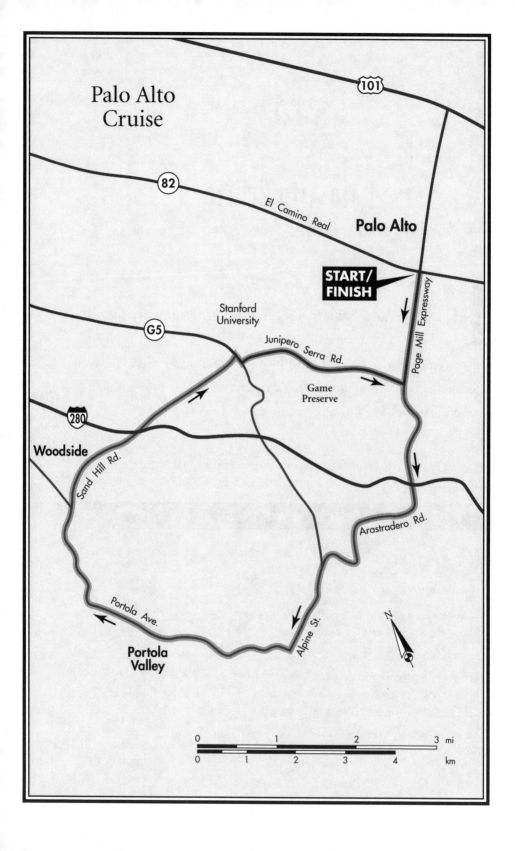

through oak chaparral and piney forests, passing by the Arastradero Park and Biological Preserve and down the Portola Valley. Neon green in spring and tawny brown in summer, the hills are often enshrouded in fog coming in from the coast.

After a hearty dose of climbing on Alpine Street and Portola Avenue, you descend back to the Silicon Valley via Sand Hill Road, which leads you by the entrance to the famed Stanford Linear Accelerator. A physicist's dream that stretches for nearly 3 miles across the landscape, the accelerator is where scientists engage in a kind of high-speed subatomic demolition derby. As your bike accelerates by this expensive test site, the Hoover Tower, a university landmark, will come into view (a sign that you are at the edge of campus). After veering onto Junipero Serra Road, you ride along a wide and pleasant thoroughfare, with the university on the left and a game refuge on the right, both harboring their own kind of wildlife or wild life. After 2.5 miles you arrive at the Page Mill Expressway intersection, which takes you back to Palo Alto Square and the ride's end.

MILES AND DIRECTIONS

0.0 West on Page Mill Expressway from Palo Alto Square Plaza.

1.3 Continue straight at intersection with Junipero Serra Road.

1.4 Begin climbing.

1.7 Summit.

2.2 Cross under Highway 280 (note separate bike lane between lanes of traffic).

2.6 Right onto Arastradero Road.

3.0 Arastradero Preserve.

4.9 Left on Alpine Street. Begin climbing.

5.9 Summit. Right on Portola Avenue (good shoulder).

6.9 Begin steep descent.

8.3 Entering Woodside.

8.9 Begin climbing.

9.3 Veer right onto Sand Hill Road.

9.7 Summit.

10.0 Begin climbing.

10.8 Summit.

11.0 Divided highway begins.

12.3 Pass Stanford Linear Accelerator Center.

13.0 Right onto Santa Cruz Avenue and then immediate left onto Junipero Serra Road. Begin descent. (Sign directs bikes to merge with autos.)

14.3 Left onto Page Mill Expressway.

15.6 Ride ends at Palo Alto Square Shopping Plaza.

Black Mountain Cruise

LOS ALTOS — MONTEBELLO OPEN SPACE PRESERVE — LOS ALTOS

W *hoa! Check out the view! San Jose is a less-than-inspiring town to ride a bike through, but it's a great place to ride above. And the Black Mountain Cruise gives you the opportunity to do just this, providing a 360-degree view that includes Silicon Valley as well as the Pacific Ocean, Mount Tamalpais, Mount Diablo, and Mount Hamilton.*

The ride starts at Bicycle Outfitter on the Foothill Expressway in Los Altos. If you hang out on Foothill for any length of time, you'll realize that you've come to road-bike heaven, as a steady stream of racers, tourists, and commuters files past. The cruise goes south on Foothill to Stevens Canyon Reservoir, where there are bathrooms.

The 5-mile climb up Montebello Road starts with a series of steep switchbacks, before entering a stream canyon. Note the Sunrise Winery and Picchetti Ranch near the bottom of the climb. Road gradients on this part of Montebello approach 15 percent.

For the final 2 miles of the climb, you are rewarded with spectacular views of San Jose and the bay. After a storm this view will be crystal clear, and on these days you can see the blimp hangars at Moffett Field. Often, however, the valley will have a morning blanket of fog. After 2,100 feet of climbing, the ride reaches the end of the pavement and a gate. Guide your bike through the narrow opening of the gate, and you're in the Montebello Open Space Preserve.

The road here is a mixture of degraded pavement and packed dirt that winds through scrub pine and manzanita thickets. The riding is easy until the

An out-of-the-saddle effort on the way up Black Mountain.

final short climb to the top of Black Mountain (2,787 feet). This last quarter mile is more "technical" and will require that you keep your weight over your back wheel for traction.

THE BASICS

Start: Bicycle Outfitter, A Street and Fremont Avenue in Los Altos along Foothill Expressway.

Length: 27.0 miles.

Terrain: Major climbing on Montebello. Four miles of dirt. Cross or mountain bike recommended. Twisty downhill on Page Mill Road and Moody Road. Beware of quarry trucks on Stevens Canyon Road.

Food: The shopping center on the corner of Springer Street and Foothill Expressway has an Andronico's Market, as well as Starbucks Coffee and Sonoma Country Bagels.

For more information: Bicycle Outfitter, 963 Fremont Avenue, Los Altos, CA 94022; (650) 948–6841.

Maps: DeLorme *Northern California Atlas and Gazetteer*, map 115; Krebs Cycle Products, *South San Francisco Bay and Monterey Bay Areas* map.

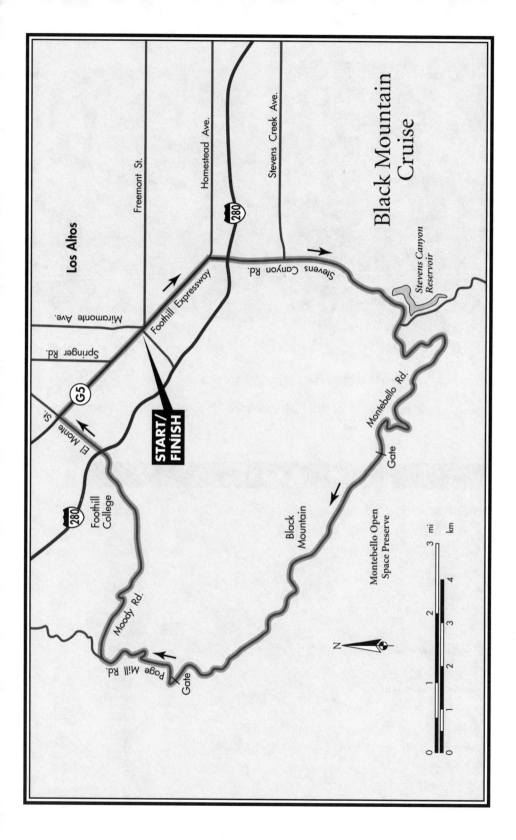

Black Mountain Cruise

0.0 Bicycle Outfitter, A Street and Fremont Avenue, Los Altos. Cross Foothill Expressway on A Street and proceed south on Foothill Expressway.

2.5 Pass under I–280.

4.5 Foothill becomes Stevens Canyon Road.

6.5 Right on Montebello Road, just past Stevens Canyon Reservoir.

11.5 Gate at the end of the pavement on Montebello.

14.0 Black Mountain.

16.0 Right on Page Mill Road. Careful on descent.

20.0 Right on Moody Road. Careful on first half-mile of the Moody downhill.

23.0 Foothill College. Go through the college at Elena Street and reconnect with El Monte Street on the other side. The road is marked here. Left on El Monte.

24.5 Right on Foothill Expressway.

27.0 Take the off-ramp from the Expressway for A Street before the underpass. Ride ends at Bicycle Outfitter, Los Altos.

The Montebello Open Space Preserve is a great area for mountain biking, with many trails going off in all directions, so expect to see some mountain bikers on this ride.

At the top of Black Mountain, you'll find an outcropping of rock on the left that is a prime viewing point for the Pacific Ocean. It's a great place to stretch out and watch the sun set over the grassy hillsides that seem to stretch forever. Below, in Stevens Canyon, runs the San Andreas Fault.

The rest of the way to Page Mill Road is downhill and somewhat loose, requiring caution on a road bike. You may want to bring along some additional clothing, as the weather can turn cold and breezy at the top, especially in the evening.

Once you reach the pavement of Page Mill and Moody Roads, you are on a typically difficult Santa Cruz Mountains descent, with one switchback after another. The top of Moody is especially hard on the neck and hands, but it then opens out into a beautiful little valley before bringing you back to the Foothill Expressway.

Santa Cruz Cruise

SANTA CRUZ — HENRY COWELL REDWOODS STATE PARK —
FELTON — SANTA CRUZ

A*s morning fog bows to the sun's penetrating rays, the forested hills that serve as backdrop to the oceanside community of Santa Cruz slowly take shape. Hidden within their furrowed flanks is a labyrinth of small roads that wind through redwood groves and sunny meadows. Though the riding options are legion in this area, many are for the stout of heart (and leg and lung). This cruise is intended for those who want to sample some of the local splendor, without overdosing on the vertical gain.*

The climbing begins almost immediately as you head out of town toward the University of California, Santa Cruz. After a brief spin along the city's avenues, you'll leave urbania behind and be engulfed in a sea of redwoods. It's a gradual uphill huff with a few downhill respites before you finally top out at mile 10. Plenty of downhill lies ahead, with the first segment following narrow and curvy Felton Empire Road. The road traverses through Henry Cowell Redwoods State Park, whose forest is as thick and wild and brown and moist as something you'd find in the Amazon. You are not, however, anywhere near the Amazon, and the small and unassuming town of Felton that waits for you at the far end of the park is your reality check.

From Felton, city life begins to thicken all around you. After you've again passed by the north boundary of Henry Cowell Redwoods State Park along Graham Hill Road, it'll be you and the cars dropping back into Santa Cruz. But

Controlled descent on the road to Santa Cruz.

this isn't necessarily a bad thing. As you descend, smell the lattes. Envision a deli sandwich and a sidewalk cafe. Click your heels three times and say, "There's no place like home." You're almost there.

THE BASICS

Start: Spokesman Bicycles at Cathcart Street near Cedar Street in downtown Santa Cruz.

Length: 20.7 miles.

Terrain: Major climbs and steep descents, few flat sections. Moderate traffic (heavy traffic in downtown Santa Cruz).

Food: There are plenty, maybe too many, food options in Santa Cruz. A natural foods grocery and several good restaurants are available in Felton.

For more information: Santa Cruz Visitors Information Center, 701 Front Street, Santa Cruz, CA 95061; (408) 425–1234. Spokesman Bicycles, 231 Cathcart Street, Santa Cruz, CA 95060; (408) 429–6062.

Maps: DeLorme *Northern California Atlas and Gazetteer,* map 115; Krebs Cycle Products, *South San Francisco Bay and Monterey Bay Areas* map.

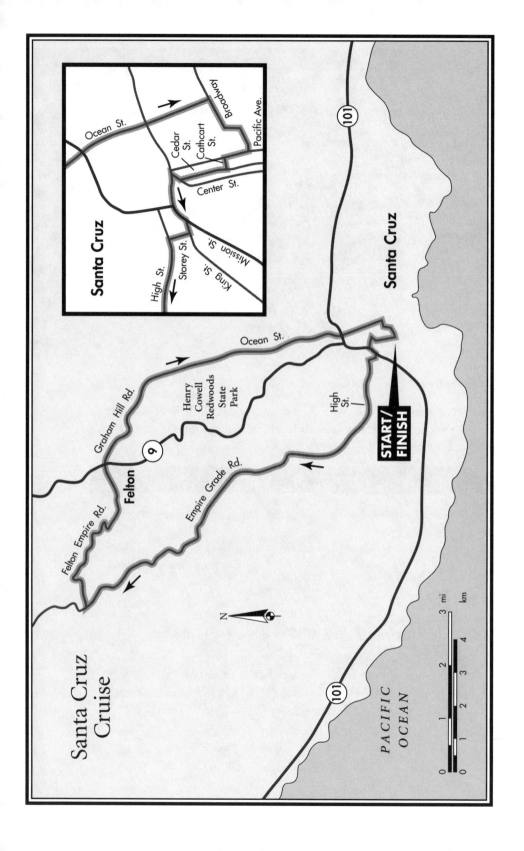

Santa Cruz
Cruise

Santa Cruz

START/
FINISH

High St.

Ocean St.

Henry
Cowell
Redwoods
State
Park

Graham Hill Rd.

Felton

9

Felton Empire Rd.

Empire Grade Rd.

N

PACIFIC
OCEAN

101

101

0   1   2   3 mi
0   1   2   3   4 km

Santa Cruz

Ocean St.

Broadway

Pacific Ave.

Cedar
St.

Cathcart
St.

Center St.

High St.

Storey St.

Mission St.

King St.

0.0 From Spokesman Bicycles on Cathcart Street in downtown Santa Cruz, proceed north on Cedar Street.

0.4 Right onto Center Street, then an immediate left onto Mission Street. Begin climbing.

0.7 Right onto King Street.

0.8 Right onto Storey Street.

1.0 Left onto High Street to UC Santa Cruz.

2.0 Pass UC Santa Cruz on the right.

3.3 Road narrows, High Street becomes Empire Grade.

6.4 Summit.

6.7 Begin climbing.

8.2 Begin steeper grade climb.

8.9 Summit.

10.0 Right on Felton Empire Road. Begin descent through Henry Cowell Redwoods State Park.

13.5 Felton.

13.6 Veer right onto Graham Hill Road (do not make the hard right onto Highway 9). Continue descent to Santa Cruz.

18.6 Santa Cruz. Graham Hill Road becomes Ocean Street.

18.8 Cross under Highway 101. Beware of traffic entering and exiting highway.

18.9 Veer right to stay on Ocean Street.

20.0 Right onto Broadway (changes to Laurel Street).

20.4 Right onto Pacific Avenue.

20.5 Left onto Cathcart Street.

20.7 Ride ends at Spokesman Bicycles on Cathcart Street.

Pebble Beach Cruise

MONTEREY — SEVENTEEN MILE DRIVE — PEBBLE BEACH
RESORT— PACIFIC GROVE — MONTEREY

Monterey and its surrounding areas have become more developed since the days of John Steinbeck, but its stunning beauty has somehow survived. It's a salty canvas painted in windswept lines and crashing waves and gentle grades leading to limitless seascape vistas. As you pedal away from the crowds of the downtown area, the dramatic coastal landscape is enough to trigger that rare, euphoric feeling of being in the best of all possible places in the best of all possible ways—on your bike.

With the vast scope of things to see and do, the 29.8-mile Pebble Beach Cruise is the kind of ride that could take all day. And maybe it should. But you're best to leave your Greg LeMond attitude behind, and instead heft along your trusty camera. This is one ride you won't want to remember as a blur.

The ride starts right outside Monterey on the edge of Roberts Lake. Within 3 miles of the ride's start, you'll reach downtown Monterey, Fisherman's Wharf, and Cannery Row. The bustling, working-class wharf of the Cannery Row that John Steinbeck made famous now exists only in the text of his classic tale. Authenticity has made way for capitalism, resulting in a 1990s tourism amalgam of McDonald's eateries, trained monkeys, and street mimes. It's a smaller-scale version of San Francisco's Fisherman's Wharf but with a bike trail.

If you can endure—maybe even get a kick out of—2 miles of true tackiness, the crowded bike path will begin to thin out and lead you to Ocean View Boulevard, one of the most sensational stretches of beach on the entire

Start: Roberts Lake parking lot. Exit Highway 1 at the Canyon Del Ray exit. Proceed under the freeway overpass and turn right on Roberts Avenue. No rest rooms in parking lot.

Length: 29.8 miles.

Terrain: Long, flat stretches and gently rolling hills. Three moderate climbs. Ultrascenic drives with fair amounts of traffic on weekends.

Food: No food mart at the ride's start, but food options galore in downtown Monterey and Carmel. For a hearty dinner at a moderate price, you might check out Rosines on Alvarado Street in downtown Monterey.

For more information: Winning Wheels, 223 Fifteenth Street, Pacific Grove, CA 93950; (408) 375-4322.

Maps: Krebs Cycle Products, *South San Francisco Bay and Monterey Bay Areas* map; Compass Maps, *Monterey Peninsula, Carmel, and Salinas–Monterey County*.

California coastline. As you cruise up the coast, make sure to unglue your eyes from the ocean long enough to check out the other side of the road, where virtually tame deer frolic on the famed Pebble Beach golf course.

After almost 4 miles of ocean, the road curves gently inland and brings you

Banking left at Carmel State Beach.

0.0 From parking lot proceed west on Roberts Avenue as it curves around the lake.

0.4 Right onto regional bike path before Delmonte Avenue.

2.3 Jog right at Washington Street to stay on path and then jog immediately left.

2.5 Enter Fisherman's Wharf, congested area.

3.7 Pass Monterey Bay Aquarium.

4.8 Right onto Ocean View Boulevard (turns into Sunset Drive).

6.1 Main residential area ends; park begins.

8.5 Right onto Seventeen Mile Drive.

9.6 Right to continue on Seventeen Mile Drive (or Spanish Bay Road).

15.7 Right to continue on Seventeen Mile Drive.

16.2 Right to continue on Seventeen Mile Drive. Begin climb.

17.8 Right following sign to Carmel Gate. Summit.

18.1 Carmel Gate.

18.4 Right onto Ocean Avenue and descend to beach.

18.5 Beach. Follow Ocean Avenue as it swings around loop and begins back uphill.

18.6 Right onto Scenic Road.

19.2 Right to continue on Scenic Road at intersection with Thirteenth Street.

19.3 Right to continue on Scenic Road.

20.0 Right to continue on Scenic Road at intersection with Isabella Road.

20.2 Pass Carmel State Beach. Scenic Road turns into Carmelo Street.

21.3 Right onto Seventh Street. Steep climb for 3 blocks.

21.5 Left onto Monte Verde Street.

21.6 Cross Ocean Avenue.

21.7 Right onto Fifth Avenue.

21.8 Left onto Dolores Street (climbing in here).

22.8 Left onto Junipero Serra Street.

22.9 Left onto Carpenter Street.

23.0 Left onto Highway 1. Summit.

23.5 Right onto Aguajito Road. Begin climb.

23.9 Summit. Begin descent.

25.0 Intersect Viejo Road; take Aguajito Road to right.

27.4 Right onto Mark Thomas Drive (bike lane) just before Highway 1.

27.5 Left onto Sloat Road (go underneath Highway).

28.0 Intersection Delmonte. Cross street and go over to bus stop and follow short trail through park to bike trail. Turn right onto bike trail.

29.4 Left onto Roberts Avenue.

29.8 Parking lot at Roberts Lake.

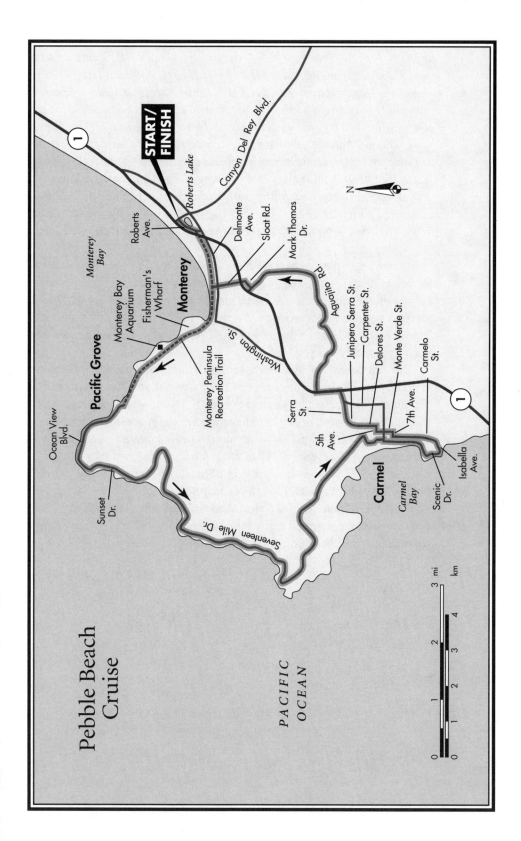

Pebble Beach
Cruise

START/
FINISH

PACIFIC
OCEAN

to the start of the Seventeen Mile Drive, which is chock-full of amazing vista points and gently rolling roads shaded by arching trees. Because this "drive" is one of the biggest tourist attractions in the entire area, you'll have to check in with a ranger and sign a waiver stating that you'll be a good bicyclist and follow the rules and stay on designated roads (sometimes the ranger may simply wave you on). Although this stretch of tarmac is hardly a secluded backroad, the overpowering grandeur of the surrounding land and sea makes it well worth the relatively minor hassle of sharing the road with car-driving tourists. And once you've experienced the two-wheeled version of this drive, with the salty wind whipping in your face and the smell of beach heather in the air, you'll feel truly sorry for all those tourists cooped up in their mechanized boxes.

As you begin the first of three climbs on this ramble, it may feel as though the road is getting narrower. At mile 16.2 a large sign warning bicyclists of the narrow shoulder confirms your suspicions that the world is closing in. Though you may begin jealously eyeing the ample, paved golf-cart lanes that run parallel to the road, take heart that most folks do drive slowly and seem more than willing to wait to pass you by.

You exit Seventeen Mile Drive at the Carmel Gate, the entryway to the extremely upscale beach town where Clint Eastwood once presided as mayor. You may want to take a break on the town's beautiful white sand beach at the end of Ocean Avenue, before heading around town on Scenic Drive. (There is also an assortment of places to eat along Ocean Avenue.) The ride out of Carmel is uphill all the way to Highway 1. A half-mile after reaching this busy road, which has a good shoulder, you begin the last of the climbs into the foothills on Aguajito Road. Though you may huff and puff on the way up, consider your reward: some of the most spectacular views of Monterey Bay. And after an awesome downhill and a bit of zigzagging, you're again back on the regional bike trail, heading to Roberts Lake.

East Bay Area

Carquinez Strait Ramble

MARTINEZ — FRANKLIN CANYON ROAD — CROCKETT —
CARQUINEZ SCENIC DRIVE — CARQUINEZ STRAIT
REGIONAL SHORELINE — MARTINEZ

Cyclists new to the sport will love the Carquinez Strait Ramble
as much as all the more-experienced local riders who have
made these delicious roads part of their regular cycling feast. On any
given day you're likely to see everyone from the buffed-legs-and-fancy-
bike set to the brand-new-bike-from-Kmart crowd out on their two-
wheeled vehicles of choice, taking advantage of the less-traveled roads.

Casual cruising up Franklin Canyon Road.

Departing from the old downtown of Martinez, you'll find it hard to believe that you'll soon be traveling amid quiet oak groves and rolling farm roads. Of course, finding your way to these glorious Bay Area backroads takes a bit of perseverance. You'll have to battle the mini-malls and golden arches of suburbia for 2 miles before your wheels roll onto the promised land. And just before you do, stop and see the incongruously located fourteen-room mansion and former home of naturalist John Muir, who lived in Martinez from 1890 to his death in 1914. Though it was once surrounded by rural splendor, Muir's home now rests in the shadow of shopping malls and a six-lane highway, the latter absurdly named the John Muir Parkway.

Franklin Canyon Road is a quiet spin that gradually ambles up for 4 miles before joining the Cummings Skyway. This latter wide-shouldered two-lane continues the journey up, offering spectacular views of San Francisco Bay. Just after the summit you peel off onto Crockett Boulevard for a gravity-fueled coast down to the town of the same name. This cafe-and-thrift-store village has a certain good-natured funk about it and serves as a kind of gateway to the 2,795-acre Carquinez Strait Regional Shoreline. This parkland is located between Crockett and the hillsides overlooking Martinez and is accessed via the appropriately named Carquinez Scenic Drive. Here you'll probably pass more walkers and cyclists than motorists.

THE BASICS

Start: Berrellesa Street and Escobar Street in Martinez.

Length: 18.8 miles.

Terrain: Rolling hills, with one extended climb. Quiet country roads for the majority of the ride. Rough conditions between Port Costa and Martinez.

Food: Grocery stores and restaurants at the ride start in Martinez and, later, in Crockett. There are also two restaurants in Port Costa.

For more information: Valley Spokesmen Bicycle Touring Club, Box 2630, Dublin, CA 94568; Bonnie Powers, (925) 828-5299; www.valleyspokesmen.org.

Maps: DeLorme *Northern California Atlas and Gazetteer,* maps 94 and 95; Krebs Cycle Products, *North San Francisco Bay and Wine Country* map.

Coastal hills that rise steeply up to 750 feet above Carquinez Strait are a mix of open, rolling grasslands, wooded ravines, eucalyptus-shaded meadows, and river shoreline. Below, huge freighters ply the narrow strait on their way to refineries and other depots upriver. At mile 12.9 you pass the turnoff for the forgotten hamlet of Port Costa, which rests hidden in a narrow cleft in the hills on the very edge of the strait. You can refuel at the Bull Valley Restaurant and Inn or peruse the antiques shops in town before pushing on.

Just after you pass the quarry operated by Pacific Custom Materials—beware of road damage here—you'll encounter a road closure. Go around the gate and continue traveling on the Carquinez Scenic Drive. The road is washed out, making it dangerous for cars but quite passable by bicycle. The absence of autos makes this short section of the route mystifyingly quiet. The fluttering of birds overhead and perhaps the whir of another bicycle wheel are the only sounds you'll hear. Watch for chunks of missing asphalt that disintegrate into dirt and for broken bits of road just waiting to puncture your tires. Your

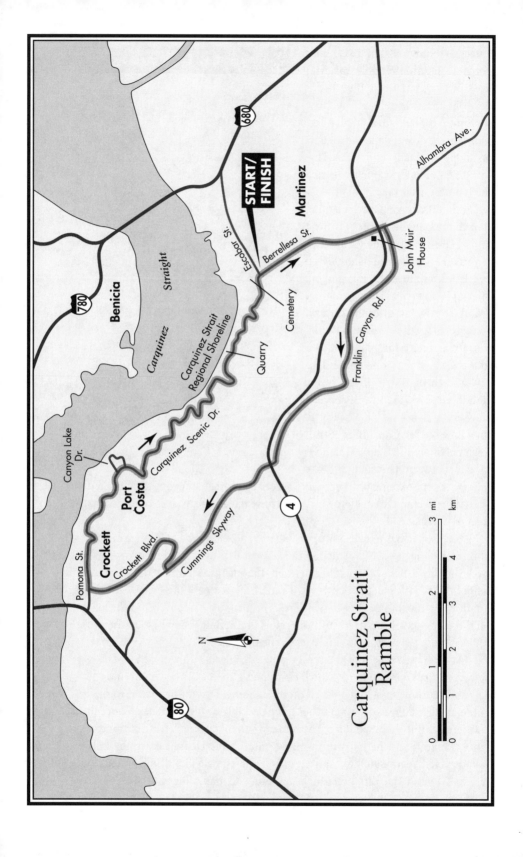

Carquinez Strait
Ramble

0.0 South on Berrellesa Street (a one-way).

0.9 Merge with Alhambra Avenue. Beware of traffic entering/exiting retail stores.

1.9 John Muir House.

2.0 Cross under Highway 4.

2.1 Right onto Franklin Canyon Road.

2.4 Begin climb.

6.4 Right on Cummings Skyway.

7.3 Summit. Begin descent.

8.6 Right on Crocket Boulevard. Begin steep, winding descent.

10.6 Right on Pomona Street, which becomes Carniquez Scenic Drive.

10.8 Begin climb.

11.1 Summit. Begin rolling serpentine curves.

12.1 Carquinez Strait Regional Shoreline Park. Begin steep descent.

12.9 Pass Canyon Lake Drive (or left for a 0.6 round-trip spur to Port Costa). Begin climb.

13.7 Summit. Road begins to get very rough.

14.6 Road-closed barrier (passable by bike).

16.7 Road open to vehicles at barrier.

18.4 St. Catherine of Siena Cemetery.

18.6 Road curves right, becomes Talbert Street.

18.7 Road curves left, becomes Escobar Street.

18.8 End at intersection of Berrellesa Street.

chances of flatting here are relatively high, and you won't want to be without your requisite tube, patch kit, and pump.

The road is open to vehicles again after 2 miles, though there are often few to be found. As you rise and fall with the gentle pitches of road back to Martinez, the rush of wind and the expansive emptiness of the soft, lumpy hills are enough to evoke a near-perfect elation. The simple beauty of these grassy knolls that roll lazily to the shores of the Carquinez Strait serves as a reminder of what's really important in life.

Mount Diablo Classic

WALNUT CREEK — CLAYTON — MORGAN TERRITORY —
DANVILLE — MOUNT DIABLO STATE PARK — WALNUT CREEK

*L*ocal tribes called it tuyshtak, *the sacred birthplace of the world where the First People lived. Spanish explorers arriving in the eighteenth century also sensed the mystery and power of this great mountain, which towers nearly 4,000 feet above the East Bay. But fearing the unknown, they associated the peak with dark forces and thus named it Diablo.*

This classic ride honors the spirit of this great mountain by circumnavigating its perimeter. It also includes a 4-mile spur to the summit, whose steep, prolonged pitches can be something of a religious experience. But don't expect a natural nirvana in circling the mountain. As condos and ranch homes have marched steadily eastward from the Bay Area, the formerly wild lands that surrounded Diablo have become suburban neighborhoods. There is one exception: Morgan Territory Regional Preserve. This 3,346-acre open space covers the mountain's southern flank. In spring the expansive grasslands of the preserve are where the rare Mount Diablo fairy lantern blooms along with other wildflowers. In summer the sinuous green foothills fade to the color of lion's fur, with temperatures hovering in the high 90s. Though the preserve is not technically a wilderness area, it certainly feels like one.

Beginning in upscale Walnut Creek—where you'll be hard pressed to find either a walnut or a creek—you'll venture through the suburban jungles of Clayton and Danville. Pedaling along four-lane Ygnacio Valley Road, you pass by brand-new housing developments, with many more likely to have been built since this text was written. Suburban Americana abruptly ends (hopefully), and the ageless beauty of the natural world begins on Marsh Creek Road, where you roll through farmland on a virtually empty stretch of tarmac. Modest farm-houses with horses grazing in the front yards are scattered about the open grasslands. The route becomes even more bucolic as you turn onto Morgan Territory Road, where gentle old trees form a shaded archway over the narrow road. The road gets continually skinnier, steeper, and more remote. Trees thicken around you. Watch out for the occasional car that may pop up unexpectedly around one of the snakey bends.

The open space of the Morgan Territory Regional Preserve is a liberating experience after a long climb in the trees, though you may soon miss the cool shadiness out in the hot sun. Near the summit you'll come to what the East Bay Regional Parks Department calls a "staging area," basically a parking lot where there are toilets and a source of drinking water. After some well-deserved downhill (beware of autos lurking around blind corners), the road widens to two lanes and becomes a flat ribbon stretching across quiet countryside.

When you reach the Danville city limits, you'll have 5 miles of suburban riding—including a cruise through the sticky-sweet gingerbread houses and tennis villas along Blackhawk Road—before turning onto Mount Diablo Scenic Drive toward Mount Diablo State Park. From here you'll have nearly 10 miles of climbing before reaching Diablo's summit. And 10 miles of relentless climbing can feel like dragging an anvil when you've already done 50 miles, especially on a hot day.

From Mount Diablo's lofty heights you can see for hundreds of miles in all directions. Immediately north and east is the Sacramento Delta, with its convoluted maze of waterways. Farther east the great Central Valley stretches to the Sierra Nevada, which hovers above the plain like a mirage. Due west is San Francisco Bay, Mount Tamalpais, and the distant Farallon Islands. North is Napa's Mount St. Helena and, on really good days, Mount Lassen in the Cascades.

But distant views are not all you become conscious of way up high.

THE BASICS

Start: Shopping plaza at the corner of Oak Grove Road and Ygnacio Valley Road in Walnut Creek.

Length: 61.5 miles.

Terrain: Much extended climbing, rolling hills, some flat sections; traffic in suburbs and towns but virtually no traffic through parklands.

Food: Restaurants and stores available at Walnut Creek shopping plaza. No food available for 30 miles between Clayton and Danville. Water fountains but no food on Mount Diablo and Morgan Territory Regional Preserve (call ahead to double-check).

For more information: Valley Spokesmen Bicycle Touring Club, P.O. Box 2630, Dublin, CA 94568; Bonnie Powers, (510) 828–5299. East Bay Regional Parks, Antioch office; (925) 757–2620. California State Parks; (925) 837–2525.

Maps: DeLorme *Northern California Atlas and Gazetteer,* map 105; Compass Maps, *Contra Costa County.*

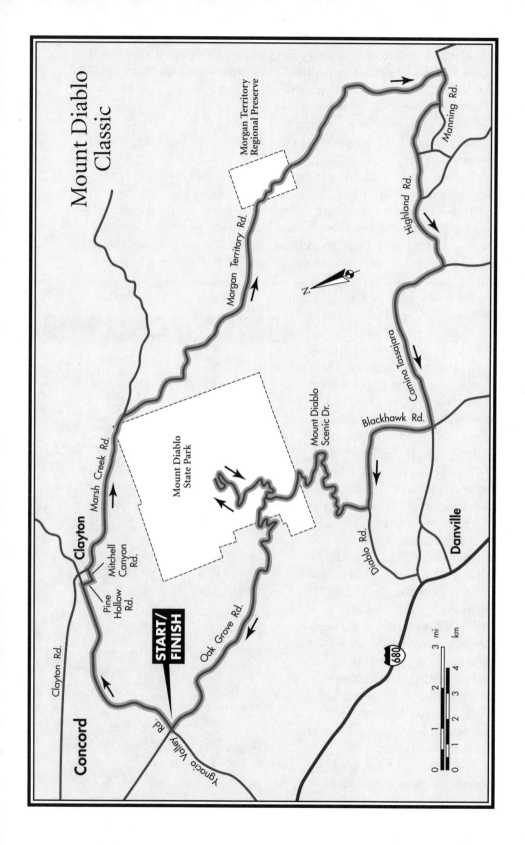

0.0 From shopping plaza at the corner of Oak Grove Road and Ygnacio Valley Road, head east on Ygnacio Valley Road.

0.6 Begin climbing.

1.6 Summit.

3.2 Right on Pine Hollow Road (residential area). Begin gradual climbing.

4.4 Summit.

4.9 Left on Mitchell Canyon Road.

5.0 Right on Clayton Road.

5.4 Right on Marsh Creek Road. Begin gradual climbing.

6.3 Right to stay on Marsh Creek Road.

7.1 Leave residential area.

9.0 Summit.

9.7 Right on Morgan Territory Road.

13.4 Begin climbing steeply.

18.8 Morgan Territory Regional Preserve staging area.

19.2 Summit.

20.2 Begin steep descent.

24.3 Right onto Manning Road.

25.1 Right onto Highland Road.

29.7 Right onto Camino Tassajara.

32.1 Pass Black Hawk Drive (entrance to Blackhawk Country Club).

32.9 Danville town limits.

34.3 Right onto Blackhawk Road.

37.6 Blackhawk Road becomes Diablo Road.

37.7 Right onto Mount Diablo Scenic Drive toward Mount Diablo State Park and Athenian School. Begin climbing.

38.7 Enter Mount Diablo State Park.

41.2 Pass park toll entrance (bikes are free). Levels off.

42.4 Begin climbing steadily.

44.2 Right to Mount Diablo summit.

47.7 Devil's Elbow hairpin.

48.6 Summit; turnaround point.

52.9 Right at intersection toward Walnut Creek.

59.2 Leave Mount Diablo State Park.

60.1 Walnut Creek town limit.

60.5 Right onto Oak Grove Road.

61.5 Ride ends at shopping plaza at intersection with Ygnacio Valley Road.

Uphill dance with the devil on Mount Diablo.

Like bats around a belfry, dragonflies swarm over Diablo's summit during the summer months. In winter and spring the peak may be covered in snow (see sidebar information for road conditions). Regardless of the season, once you've reached the top, the pain of the climb is superseded by the victory of the conquest. And as the wind blows through your sweaty hair, you can look forward to the promise of 11 miles of scenic descending back to Walnut Creek. The bottom of Diablo ends in a beautiful straightaway, which provides the perfect finish to an epic journey.

Bear Creek Cruise

ORINDA — BEAR CREEK ROAD — BRIONES RESERVOIR — ALHAMBRA
VALLEY ROAD — SAN PABLO RESERVOIR — ORINDA

The commuter rail line known as BART (Bay Area Rapid Transit) pops through the eastern slope of the Berkeley Hills near Orinda, one of several upscale villages in the East Bay. The town itself is nondescript, but beyond its limits lies one of the more popular loop rides in the Bay Area.

The Bear Creek Cruise, also known as the Three Bears Loop, is a casual jaunt through the hills and valleys of part of the East Bay Municipal Water District Watershed, a large tract of undeveloped forest and grassland that includes the Briones and San Pablo reservoirs. The ride attracts both racers and casual tourists alike, all in search of soothing scenery and a satisfying workout. (The route is part of the annual Berkeley Hills Road Race sponsored by the Berkeley Bike Club). Some of the riders you'll see on this loop climbed up and over the hills from Berkeley or El Cerrito via Wildcat Canyon Road, others came from nearby Pleasant Hill or Lafayette, while still others may have traveled from more distant parts on BART, with bikes in tow.

Regardless of how you get there, this cruise is worth the trip. It starts at the Orinda Village Center in downtown Orinda. From there you head north along the busy but bike-laned Camino Pablo, passing the Orinda Country Club golf course before reaching the Bear Creek Road turnoff at 1.5 miles. Here you leave most of the traffic behind and head for the hills.

After an initial short downhill on Bear Creek, you begin the longest climb of the route. The road slowly rises for nearly 3 miles, offering great views of San Pablo and Briones Reservoirs to the north and east and the often fog-enshrouded Berkeley Hills to the west. After that it's a roller-coaster ride for another

Start: Orinda Village Center at Camino Pablo and Camino Sobrante.

Length: 21.4 miles.

Terrain: Rolling hills, with one extended climb. Quiet country roads and busier thoroughfares interspersed through the ride.

Food: Grocery stores and restaurants at the ride start in Orinda.

For more information: Berkeley Bike Club, P.O. Box 817, Berkeley, CA 94701; www.berkeleybike.org. Valley Spokesmen Bicycle Touring Club, Box 2630, Dublin, CA 94568; Bonnie Powers, (925) 828–5299; www.valleyspokesmen.org. San Francisco Bay Area Rapid Transit District, P.O. Box 12688, Oakland CA 94606-2688; (415) 989–2278; www.bart.gov.

Maps: DeLorme *Northern California Atlas and Gazetteer,* maps 104 and 105; Krebs Cycle Products, *North San Francisco Bay and Wine Country* map.

3 miles, leaving the watershed area briefly and passing Bottomly Farm Stables, before descending steeply to the Alhambra Valley Road intersection. The road levels off here and heads steadily northwest to Castro Ranch Road. You now begin your reentry to a more-populated world. After a brief climb you glide down to San Pablo Dam Road and begin the long, smooth return to Orinda. At mile 19.9 you pass the Bear Creek Road intersection once again. Now you can casually cruise back to Orinda, or you can turn left onto Bear Creek for another lap on the loop. As far as this ride is concerned, once is not always enough.

Fog and power lines hover over the climb on Bear Creek Road.

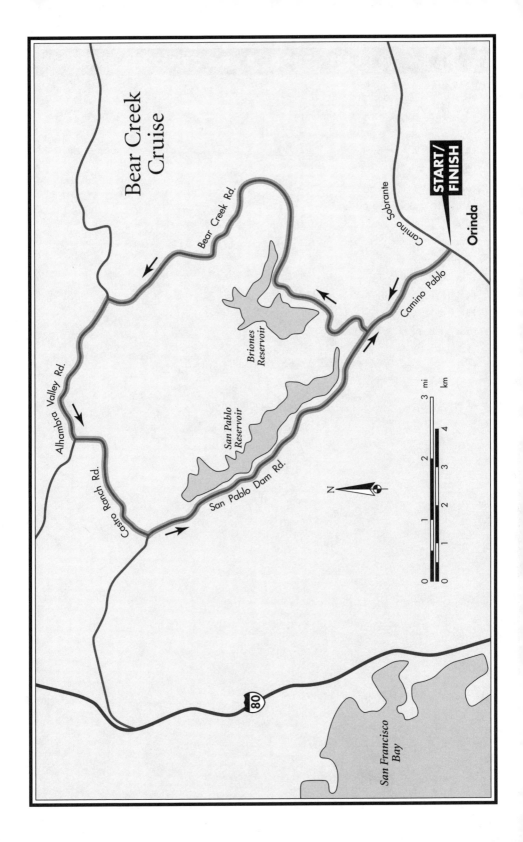

0.0 North on Camino Pablo.

1.5 Right onto Bear Creek Road.

1.7 Begin climb (brief reprieve at mile 4).

4.5 Summit. Begin descent.

5.5 Begin climb.

6.4 Summit.

7.6 Begin steep descent.

9.7 Left onto Alhambra Valley Road.

12.4 Left onto Castro Ranch Road.

12.9 Richmond city limit.

13.8 Begin steep descent.

14.6 Left onto San Pablo Dam Road.

15.0 Begin climb.

15.8 View of San Pablo Reservoir.

15.9 Summit.

19.9 Pass Bear Creek Road on left. (San Pablo Dam Road becomes Camino Pablo.)

21.4 End at Orinda Village Center at Camino Sobrante.

Lake Chabot Challenge

MORAGA — SAN LEANDRO RESERVOIR — ANTHONY CHABOT
REGIONAL PARK — CASTRO VALLEY — LAKE CHABOT —
SKYLINE BOUELVARD — MORAGA

M any of the best loop rides consist of mixed surfaces and may include smooth, pristine pavement along with pot-holed and rutted jeep road. Such variability is the price we must some-times pay to see all that we want to see on a ride, without having to see it all again on the way back. If only there were a bike fairy who could wave her magic wand and transform our knobby-tired trail machines into feathery road bikes as we transition from dirt to tarmac, wouldn't we be grateful.

The Lake Chabot Challenge around Anthony Chabot Regional Park is one of those rides, like others in this book, which is part pavement and part dirt. The park, which covers nearly five thousand acres, is an island of green trees and blue water surrounded by a crowded urban landscape. Most of the ride fol-lows hilly asphalt grades around and through the park and is perfect for a fancy road frame. But there's also 2.5 miles of trail riding around the lakeshore on dirt trail. This is fun stuff for someone on a well-equipped bike possessing basic rough-road skills. I wouldn't suggest taking your fancy frame or race wheels here but instead recommend a semi-slicked mountain bike or cross-bike. The trail's adobe surface is dusty in summer and muddy in winter; it's a steep roller coaster with gorgeous views of the lake.

Beginning in Moraga, home of St. Mary's College and the Hearst Art Gallery, you're soon out of town and into the woods and watershed of the East Bay Municipal Utility District. Canyon Road, the first leg of the route, is narrow,

Trail segment around Lake Chabot.

and the traffic can be fast (a bike trail is available for the first half mile). But as you turn off onto Pinehurst Road, the cars thin, and San Leandro Reservoir comes into focus. The climb up Pinehurst lasts for more than a mile and then descends to Redwood Road, where your climb continues up the San Leandro hills and Anthony Chabot Park. Redwood Road winds along the summit of the hills for several miles, before plunging down to the Castro Valley. After picking your way through more neighborhoods via Seven Hills Road (there are two short but very steep ones among the seven) and busy but well-shouldered Lake Chabot Road, you turn into the marina and begin the trail ride.

The first leg is on West Shore Trail, a rolling, paved path that is popular with walkers and joggers. The dirt begins at the turnoff for Bass Cove Trail just beyond the dam, which offers steep but short pitches to climb and descend. After veering onto the Goldenrod Trail, you'll come to a short paved section, which you share with golf carts from the nearby municipal golf course. But after only a half-mile you're in the dirt again, climbing up an exposed ridge overlooking the valley below.

You intersect Skyline Boulevard

THE BASICS

Start: Moraga Center Shopping Plaza at intersection of Moraga Road, Canyon Road, and Moraga Way in Moraga.

Length: 30.8 miles.

Terrain: Hilly, with some short, flat sections around Lake Chabot. Light-trafficked roads for the majority of the ride, moderate traffic on Canyon Road leaving Moraga, Redwood Road entering Castro Valley, and Lake Chabot Road leaving Castro Valley. Dirt-trail riding part way around Lake Chabot. Cross or mountain bike recommended.

Food: Terzetto Cuisine Cafe, Moraga Center Shopping Plaza; (925) 376–3832. Grocery stores also at the ride start in Moraga. Marina Cafe at Lake Chabot (mile 15.3) has sandwiches, snacks, and drinks, but their hours of operation vary through the year; (510) 247–2526; www.norcalfishing.com/chabot.html.

For more information: Valley Spokesmen Bicycle Touring Club, Box 2630, Dublin, CA 94568; Bonnie Powers, (925) 828–5299; www.valleyspokesmen.org. Chabot Café and Marina (510) 247–2526; www.norcalfishing.com/chabot.html.

Maps: DeLorme Northern California Atlas and Gazetteer, map 105; Compass Maps, Oakland.

at mile 19.6 and begin climbing again. After the initial climb, Skyline rolls the rest of the way to Redwood Road, taking you past gorgeous homes with multi-multi-million-dollar views of the Bay Area. Redwood Road offers more than 2 miles of downhill and shady relief to Pinehurst Road, where you have one more mile-long moderate climb before the coast back to Moraga on Canyon. Once in Moraga grab a latte at the Terzetto Cuisine Cafe, where you can ponder the many nuances of road and trail travel.

San Francisco Bay glimmers in the afternoon sun as seen from Skyline Boulevard.

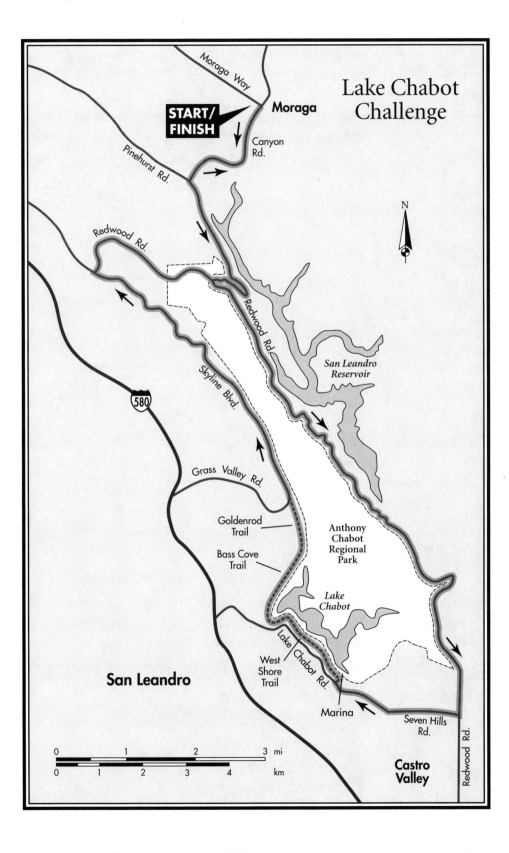

Lake Chabot Challenge

Moraga

START/FINISH

Moraga Way

Canyon Rd.

Pinehurst Rd.

Redwood Rd.

N

Redwood Rd.

San Leandro Reservoir

580

Skyline Blvd.

Grass Valley Rd.

Goldenrod Trail

Bass Cove Trail

Anthony Chabot Regional Park

Lake Chabot

West Shore Trail

Lake Chabot Rd.

Marina

San Leandro

Seven Hills Rd.

Redwood Rd.

Castro Valley

0   1   2   3 mi

0   1   2   3   4 km

0.0 Head south on Canyon Road from the Moraga Center Shopping Plaza at intersection of Moraga Road, Canyon Road, and Moraga Way in Moraga.

0.6 Road narrows at bridge crossing. Bike route available on left immediately after bridge through gate.

1.6 Leave Moraga town limits.

1.8 Left onto Pinehurst Road.

1.9 Begin climbing.

3.2 Summit.

4.4 Left onto Redwood Road.

5.7 Begin climbing.

6.2 Anthony Chabot Regional Park.

7.6 Summit.

12.3 Golf Course entrance on right. Begin climbing.

13.0 Summit. Entering Castro Valley residential area.

13.5 Right onto Seven Hills Road (two steep short climbs ahead).

14.1 Veer right onto busy Lake Chabot Road.

15.1 Right into Lake Chabot Park and Marina. After passing entrance kiosk veer right onto West Shore trail before parking lot toward Marina Cafe and boat rental.

17.0 Cross dam.

17.1 Right onto Bass Cove Trail (begin unpaved trail section).

18.1 Veer left onto Goldenrod Trail.

18.6 Right where pavement begins on Goldenrod Trail (beware of golf carts).

18.7 Right on unpaved Goldenrod Trail (at powerline tower). Paved golf-cart trail continues straight to golf course.

19.5 Veer left at water fountain and descend to Skyline Boulevard.

19.6 Trail ends at Grass Valley Staging Area. Veer right onto Skyline Boulevard. Begin climbing.

21.2 Divided road begins.

22.3 Summit. Continue rolling hills.

24.0 Right onto Redwood Road. Begin long descent.

26.4 Left onto Pinehurst Road. Begin climbing.

27.6 Summit.

29.0 Right on Canyon Road.

30.8 Ride ends at Moraga Center Shopping Plaza.

Sierra Nevada/
Central Valley

Chico to Paradise Challenge

CHICO — PARADISE — HONEY RUN ROAD —
BIDWELL PARK — CHICO

T he town of Chico lies nestled amid fiery canyons and undulat-
ing country roads so unassuming, yet home to Chico State
University, the so-called bad-boy party school of California's higher education system. But don't let the media fool you. Cyclists in the know have
long flocked to Chico for its small-town charm, quiet country roads, and,
of course, to hoist a few cool ones at the Sierra Nevada Brewery, which
churns out one of the best local beers in the state. One look around at all
the buffed legs and cool bikes in Chico and you'll understand why some
visiting cyclists loved it so much that they never left.

Your ride begins in downtown Chico on Second Street, at North Rim
Adventure Sports, a charming shop that is very helpful to cyclo-tourists.
(Riders wishing to explore other interesting bike shops will find several within
a few blocks of the starting point. Chico is a very bike-friendly town.)

The Chico to Paradise Challenge is blessed with all the qualities that make
for a perfect ride: the peace and solitude of less-traveled roads, varying terrain,
incredible scenery, and a swooping daredevil descent that twists down one of
the most gorgeous roads in all of America. If you're visiting Chico in summer,
you'll want to do this ride in the early morning or late afternoon: Temperatures
can easily soar above 100 degrees in the warm months.

The first half of your ride is pancake-flat. You'll coast through shaded
orchards and open farmland as the distant canyonlands draw nearer. With each
passing mile their fiery hues become more brilliant—and their summits appear
even steeper.

After 19 miles of relative coasting, the climbing begins. If you can handle the 4-mile uphill grind, you'll enter Paradise, a tiny hilltop town whose name is only slightly euphemistic. From there you'll follow roller-coaster hills to Honey Run Road, where a descent of fearful proportions awaits. This six-mile plummet—not recommended for the neophyte rider—is the granddaddy of highlights in a ride chock-full of mini-thrills. The road leads to a covered bridge (currently being repaired) at Butte Creek, and you're likely to find other cyclists hanging out and taking in the view here before heading back to the confines of civilization. From the bridge a quick ride takes you to the wooded trails of Bidwell Park, which will lead you back to downtown Chico. Here all the creature comforts necessary to fully bask in aprés-ride glow are right around the corner.

Chico officers on patrol. (Courtesy Chico Police Department)

THE BASICS

Start: North Rim Adventure Sports, 178 East Second Street (near Wall Street) in downtown Chico.

Length: 46.5 miles.

Terrain: Nineteen miles of flat farmland on quiet country roads. One extended climb; one lengthy and exceptionally bumpy, steep descent. Exercise caution!

Food: Chico Natural Foods offers a great selection of organic produce and healthful snacks. There is a convenience store on the route in Paradise. Back in Chico the food options abound.

For more information: Chico Velo Cycling Club, P.O. Box 2285, Chico, CA 95927; (530) 343–VELO. North Rim Adventure Sports, 178 East Second Street, Chico, CA 95928; (530) 345–2453.

Maps: DeLorme *Northern California Atlas and Gazetteer*, maps 67 and 68; Compass Maps, *Chico, Oroville, Paradise, and Butte County.*

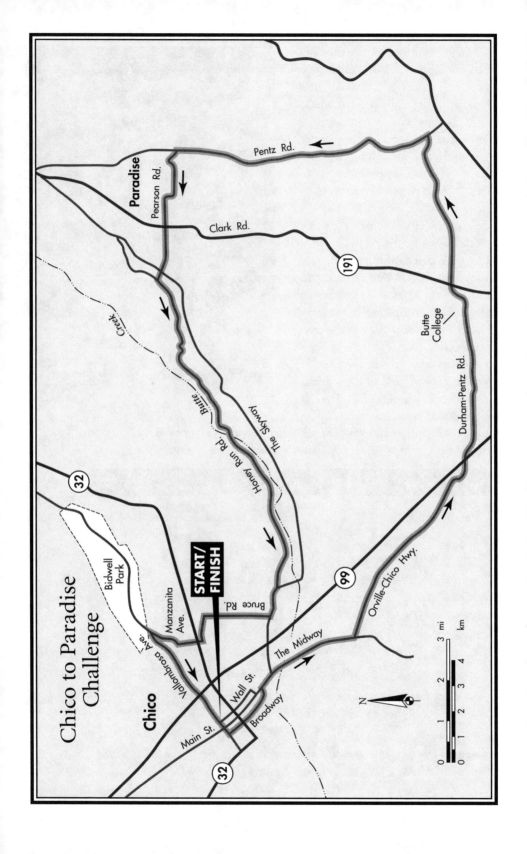

MILES AND DIRECTIONS

0.0 From North Rim Adventure Sports, take Second Street west.

0.1 Left on Broadway.

0.2 Left onto Oroville Avenue.

0.3 Veer right on Park Avenue.

1.5 Park Avenue and East Park Avenue intersect; continue straight. Park Avenue becomes The Midway. (Look for bike path that parallels The Midway.)

3.9 Veer left onto Oroville-Chico Highway. *Careful:* It's easy to miss.

8.9 Oroville-Chico Highway ends at Durham-Dayton Highway. Left onto Durham-Dayton Highway (99).

9.4 Cross over Highway 99; becomes Durham-Pentz Road.

13.2 Butte College.

18.2 Durham-Pentz Road ends at Pentz Road. Left onto Pentz Road.

19.0 Climb begins.

23.8 Paradise city limits; food and water available.

25.0 Left onto Pearson Road; roller-coaster hills—have fun!

28.5 Pearson Road ends at The Skyway. Turn right onto The Skyway.

28.6 Left onto Honey Run Road. *Caution:* Steep and bumpy descent on twisty one-lane road. Wear gloves and watch for cars.

32.2 Honey Run Road widens to two lanes.

34.3 Single-lane bridge at Butte Creek (beware of oncoming vehicles). Veer left and continue on Honey Run Road.

38.7 Right onto The Skyway. Back to civilization.

39.5 Right onto Bruce Road; Bruce Road becomes Centennial Avenue, then Chico Canyon Road, then Manzanita Avenue.

42.9 Left onto Vallombrosa Avenue.

46.0 Vallombrosa Avenue becomes Second Street.

46.5 Ride ends at North Rim Adventure Sports.

Davis Cruise

DAVIS — PUTAH CREEK ROAD — WINTERS —
RUSSELL BOULEVARD — DAVIS

T he town of Davis has embraced cycling like few others. It was the first city in the United States to establish a comprehensive citywide system of bike lanes, it recently opened a bicycle museum, and even the town logo is made from the image of an old highwheeler. Better yet, there are hundreds of cyclists on the roads. According to the city bike coordinator, as many as one thousand bikes pass by per hour at some busy intersections when the University of California is in session.

But that's not all. In May bike fans come out for a weeklong gala, appropriately name Cyclebration, in honor of the spoked machine and all it has to offer. In the past the event featured free showings of the classic movie *Breaking Away* and culminated in a Sunday morning highwheeler race.

Like other great bike cities of the world, Davis is frying-pan flat—and often as hot. Beyond the city limits the Central Valley plain stretches from the Sierras to the Vaca Mountains. Here you'll find carefully tilled fields sliced into surgically straight rows and planted in a host of different crops. Sunflowers are common; the area supplies the seed used to grow most of the sunflower crop in the Midwest. Beginning in mid-July these great plants march by the road in beautiful columns, their heads hanging wearily toward the ground. They are often your only company out on the quiet roads.

From the ride's start at the Espresso Roma Cafe, you'll take the bike lane along Third Street to the edge of campus and pick up the separate bike path that will take you out of town under a canopy of shady trees. At mile 6.5 the bike path ends. You then segue to the first of several lightly traveled country roads.

Start: Espresso Roma Cafe (231 East Street, just south of Third and E Streets).

Length: 39.1 miles.

Terrain: Flat farm roads. Generally light traffic, heavier on Roads 89 and 99. Beware of farm trucks.

Food: Many restaurants in downtown Davis. Also worth a visit is the Davis Food Co-op at Sixth and G Streets. There are grocery stores and an assortment of cafes and restaurants in Winters.

For more information: Davis Bike Club, 336 Del Oro, Davis, CA 95616; DBC Hotline, (530) 756–0186. Wheelworks Bike Shop, Third Street and F Street, Davis, CA 95616; (530) 753–3118.

Maps: DeLorme *Northern California Atlas and Gazetteer,* map 85; Compass Maps, *Davis-Woodland.*

After passing over Putah Creek Bridge—painted in colorful graffiti swashes—you turn right onto unmarked Putah Creek Road. Compared with the other sections, this is the curvy part of the route, thanks to the snakey shape of nearby Putah Creek.

Cross Putah Creek again, after turning right, and you're rolling into the farming community of Winters, a small and welcoming town with a few sincere restaurants, a large feed-and-seed store, and less than a dozen blocks of modest homes.

From Winters the road heads soberly north in clear sight of the Vaca Mountains. Traffic is a little heavier here. A stoic white barn marks the turn onto Road 27—no real need for cutesy names like

Highwheelers take to the streets during Davis's annual Cyclebration.

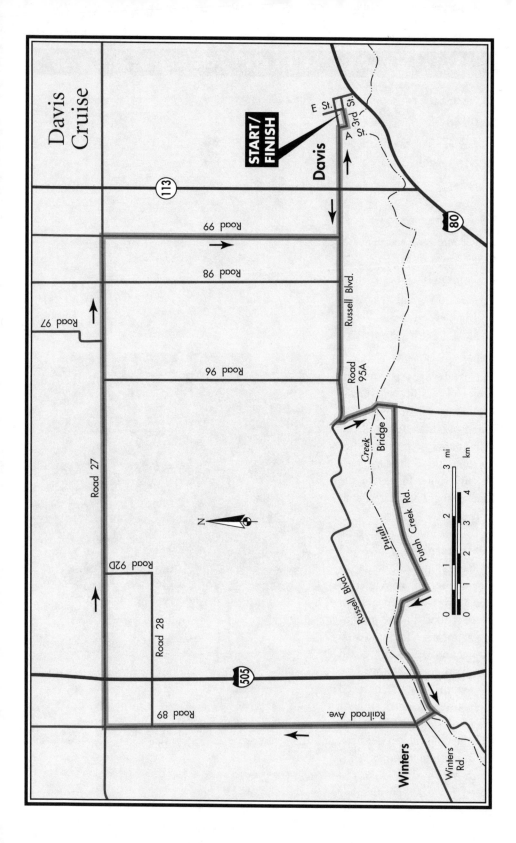

0.0 West on Third Street from Third and E Streets.

0.2 Vehicle barricade.

0.4 Right onto A Street; bike path available on west side of road.

0.5 Left along Russell Boulevard (bike path turns left at Russell).

1.6 Cross over Highway 113.

6.5 Bike path ends at three-way intersection; sharp left onto Road 95A (road sign is difficult to see).

7.1 Cross graffiti-covered Putah Creek Bridge.

7.8 Right onto Putah Creek Road (unmarked).

11.7 Road curves to right.

13.8 Cross under overpass.

14.7 Right onto Winters Road at stop sign (toward Winters). Cross Putah Creek bridge.

14.8 Enter Winters. Winters Road becomes Railroad Avenue and eventually becomes Road 89.

21.6 Right onto Road 27.

22.5 Cross Highway 505.

31.4 Right onto Road 99.

36.0 Davis city limits.

36.4 Left onto Russell Boulevard; bike path on south side of road.

37.5 Cross Highway 113.

38.6 Right onto A Street along bike path.

38.7 Left onto Third Street.

39.1 End at Third and E Streets.

Almond Orchard Avenue out here. To get back to Davis, just count the road names (96, 97, 98, 99) and periodically make right turns.

From the intersection with Road 99, you'll have 8 more flat miles back to Davis. When you reach the bike path along Russell Boulevard, you retrace the first leg of the ride back into town.

Interested in a longer route? Ask a salesperson in one of the local bike shops about the Davis Double, sponsored by the Davis Bike Club. This well-attended group ride, held during Cyclebration Week, traverses hill and dale for 200 miles, with riders completing it all in about fifteen hours or less. It is a ride you'll not soon forget. Ouch!

Folsom Challenge

FOLSOM — AMERICAN RIVER BIKE TRAIL — AUBURN —
COOL — PILOT HILL — SALMON FALLS ROAD — FOLSOM

I*n the oft-divisive cycling world, some persons see bike paths as the blessed, two-wheeled solution to overcrowded city streets, whereas others view them as part of a mastermind conspiracy to keep bicycles off the road. Are bike riders being handed the recycled rhetoric of the pre–civil rights, down-South, separate-but-equal dogma? Or do we even want to share the roads with smelly, obnoxious cars?*

This ride provides a bit of both. The Folsom Challenge offers a beautiful bike trail, followed by 20 miles of scenic but well-traveled highway, followed by 20 miles of twisting country roads, before finally returning to the suburbs. Beginning at Bicycles Plus in Folsom, you are soon riding along the American River on a bike trail. At the end of the pavement, at Beal's Point, there are rest rooms and water. This is the upper part of the Jedediah Smith Bicycle Trail, featured as another ride in this book. (See the American River Bike Trail Ramble in this chapter.)

The bike path so far has paralleled Auburn-Folsom Road, which you will turn onto at the Folsom Lake Park entrance road. From here you'll have to deal with cars and hills as you make your way to Auburn, but the scenery along the tree-lined road is relaxing, with the white fences of horse ranches bordering the road and the ornate gates of ritzy planned communities popping up every now and then. For most of its length, Auburn-Folsom has a wide shoulder that will serve as a bike lane.

Canoeists ply the American River near Rainbow Bridge.

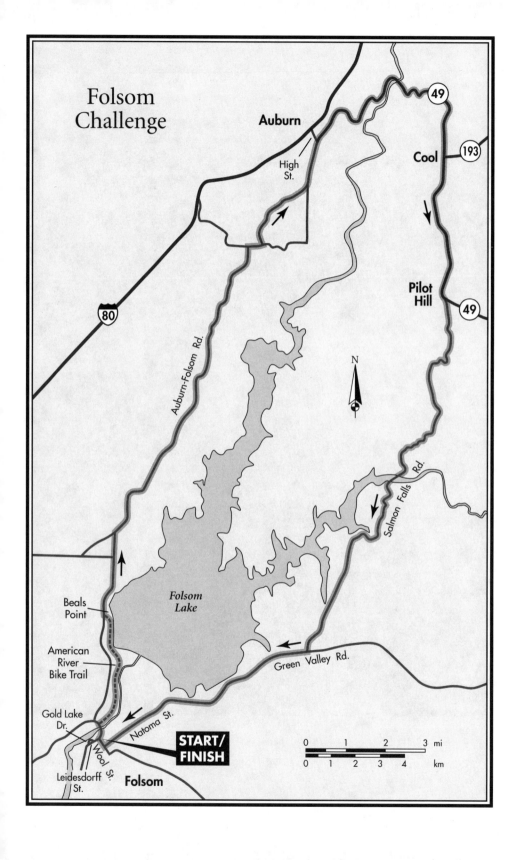

Folsom Challenge

Auburn

High St.

Cool

Pilot Hill

49

193

49

80

N

Auburn-Folsom Rd.

Salmon Falls Rd.

Folsom Lake

Beals Point

American River Bike Trail

Green Valley Rd.

Gold Lake Dr.

Natoma St.

Wool St.

START/ FINISH

Leidesdorff St.

Folsom

| 0 | 1 | 2 | 3 mi |

| 0 | 1 | 2 | 3 | 4 km |

After 20 miles of riding and a thousand feet of climbing, you reach Auburn, a quaint Gold Rush community now becoming a suburb of Sacramento. Auburn is worth a visit on its own, and a few loops around the downtown section will reveal quite a collection of nineteenth-century architecture. Leaving Auburn on Highway 49, you are immediately plunged into the wilds of the American River canyon. The descent here is smooth, fast, and banked, so save your sightseeing for the bottom, where you are treated to a view of the famous Forest Hill Bridge high above you.

From here there's nowhere to go but up. After following Highway 49 across the American River, you'll be faced with a steep and writhing climb up a skinny road cut deep into the side of the mountain. Shoulders are virtually nonexistent here, and there are a few serious blind spots, so ascend with utmost caution (and always ride single file). Although the climb is only 2 miles, the top comes just in the nick of time for most legs. From here the foliage becomes greener, and the road transcends from a harsh, mountain-hugging challenge to a rollicking romp through pleasantly rolling fields.

These gentle hills mark your entrance into the tiny town of Cool (don't you want to live there?), where you can get a snack at the general store and be on your way. This blink-and-you'll-miss-it burg boasts beautiful, vast pastureland and only a few slight buildings. There's not much to do out here except ride, which, of course, makes the riding near-perfect. You'll roll along for 4 more miles before hitting Pilot Hill and turning off, right after the gas station, onto the unmarked Salmon Falls Road. After dealing with one more brief climb, you'll be treated to miles of luscious, uninterrupted descending through verdant hillsides thick with trees and rust-colored canyons. Gorgeous valley vistas greet you around almost every bend. Salmon Falls Road typifies cycling at its flawless, inspiring best: Roads like this renew cyclists' passion for the sport and invigorate our souls.

You'll have 10 miles of countryside before plopping down in the outskirts of Folsom. And at mile 48 you'll pass Folsom Prison—the same one that

THE BASICS

Start: Bicycles Plus, 705 Gold Lake Drive; a friendly, high-quality bike shop.

Length: 50 miles.

Terrain: Steep climbs, lots of rollers and gentle uphill grades, some flat sections; moderate to heavy traffic for 2-mile climb on Highway 49 and on Auburn-Folsom Road.

Food: Coffee Republic, a nice cafe, is at the start. Various stores are located in Auburn. Convenience stores are in Cool and Pilot Hill. Nothing between Pilot Hill and Folsom.

For more information: Bicycles Plus, 705 Gold Lake Drive, Folsom, CA 95630; (916) 355-8901.

Maps: DeLorme Northern California Atlas and Gazetteer, map 87.

0.0 From Bicycles Plus, 705 Gold Lake Drive, head north for 100 yards and turn right onto the American River bike trail.

0.1 Cross the narrow old Rainbow Bridge on the bike trail.

5.4 Bike path veers right to Beal's Point. Rest rooms, water available. Turn left on entrance road to Folsom Lake State Recreation Area and leave the park.

5.7 Right onto Auburn-Folsom Road.

17.5 Auburn city limits.

20.4 Right onto High Street.

21.4 High Street becomes El Dorado (Highway 49). Begin twisty descent.

23.7 Turn right onto bridge at bottom of descent; follow sign to Cool.

23.8 Begin steep climb.

25.7 Summit.

27.1 Cool city limits.

30.6 Pilot Hill. Go straight past Rattlesnake Bar Road and Pilot Hill gas station.

31.0 Right onto Salmon Falls Road (unmarked).

31.1 Left at stop sign.

42.8 Right onto Green Valley Road.

45.8 Right onto Natoma Street.

48.0 Folsom State Prison.

49.0 Right onto Wool Street.

49.8 Left onto Leidesdorff Street.

49.9 Right onto Gold Lake Drive.

50.0 Ride ends at Bicycles Plus.

Johnny Cash made famous with "Folsom Prison Blues." Don't loiter for long along this stretch of road, lest prison authorities misconstrue your intentions. From here it's a quick ride back to the beginning through historic Folsom. At the bottom of the hill on Riley Street is the old town, home of antiques shops as well as some interesting restaurants.

American River Bike Trail Ramble

OLD SACRAMENTO — FAIR OAKS — FOLSOM —
FAIR OAKS — OLD SACRAMENTO

I*n the midst of one of America's major metropolitan areas lies 32 miles of parkway bike path that promises many pleasant rides to cyclists of all levels. This is the American River Bike Trail, which goes from Old Sacramento along the Sacramento River to Beal's Point on Folsom Lake.*

Formally known as the Jedediah Smith Bicycle Trail, the final leg of the bike path was completed in 1985. But much earlier a similar trail ran along the river to Folsom. Built in 1896 by the Capital City Wheelmen, this path was a wildly popular cinder track in its day. Although it eventually fell into disuse, the American River Bike Trail was resurrected in 1967 as part of the American River Parkway. The bike trail is now an integral part of one of the largest metropolitan parks in America.

There are many places to access the bike trail, but we will start in the most picturesque—Old Sacramento, a restoration of the town during the Gold Rush. Consisting of about one hundred buildings built between 1849 and 1876, Old Sac now also features numerous coffee shops and restaurants that make it a good place to begin and end a ride. For those persons inclined to tour without a bike, Old Sacramento also has the wonderful California Railroad Museum and the Discovery Museum, a museum of science and natural history.

From Old Sacramento the bike trail heads north through Discovery Park, passing over the American River on the Discovery Park Bridge. This bridge once stretched between Oakland and Alameda Island in San Francisco Bay and was removed piece by piece to its present site in the 1920s.

The American River Bike Trail skirts the river's edge.

Throughout its length, the bike trail is two lanes and roughly 10 feet wide, with dirt paths for runners and equestrians on either side. Mileage markers are painted on the trail, starting at Discovery Park. Speed limits on the bike path are 15 mph, and since roughly half a million cyclists ride the trail each year, this is a speed we would recommend, particularly on summer weekends.

Leaving Discovery Park, the trail goes west through a vast area of dense blackberry brambles, towering valley oaks, and fields of star thistle. On the left, behind the blackberries, is an archery complex. On the right, in the distance, is the Sacramento skyline. And you can almost imagine a time when huge forests of cottonwood and valley oak lined the American River.

Farther on you will pass ponds and sloughs populated by beavers, deer, herons, and ducks. This relatively unspoiled natural area manages to coexist only a few minutes from the city and provides interesting nature-watching in any season.

THE BASICS

Start: Old Sacramento, along the river in downtown Sacramento. Ample parking is available.

Length: 64 miles if you ride the entire trail out and back, but this route can be divided into many smaller rambles.

Terrain: Flat except for the last few miles to Folsom Lake. Some bicycle traffic. Route occasionally crosses busy roadways.

Food: Many interesting restaurants are located in Old Sacramento. Fair Oaks and Folsom offer a variety of restaurants and convenience stores.

For more information: The Rest Stop, 3230 Folsom Boulevard, Sacramento, CA 95816; (916) 453–1870. The Rest Stop has a good map selection, including the official American River Parkway map. Sacramento County Parks, 3711 Branch Center Road, Sacramento, CA 95827; (916) 875–6961. American River Parkway Foundation; (916) 456–7423.

Maps: DeLorme Northern California Atlas and Gazetteer, maps 86 and 87; Krebs Cycle Products, Lake Tahoe and Gold Country map.

Leaving behind these large wild areas, the trail passes by the Campus Commons Golf Course and reaches Sacramento State University. If you are planning a shorter ride, this is a good place to stop. The Cobblestone Cafe across from the Guy West Bridge on University Avenue offers a varied menu in pleasant outdoor surroundings. To return from here it is possible to shortcut back through the city (take M Street once you cross the J Street underpass). Downtown Sacramento is a very bike-friendly town to ride in, with wide, shady streets and lots of bike lanes.

The trail, however, continues another 20 miles before reaching Folsom Lake. Goethe Park at mile 15 has water and bathrooms. At mile 20, in Fair Oaks, riders can cross the Bridge Street Bridge and take a short side trip into old Fair Oaks.

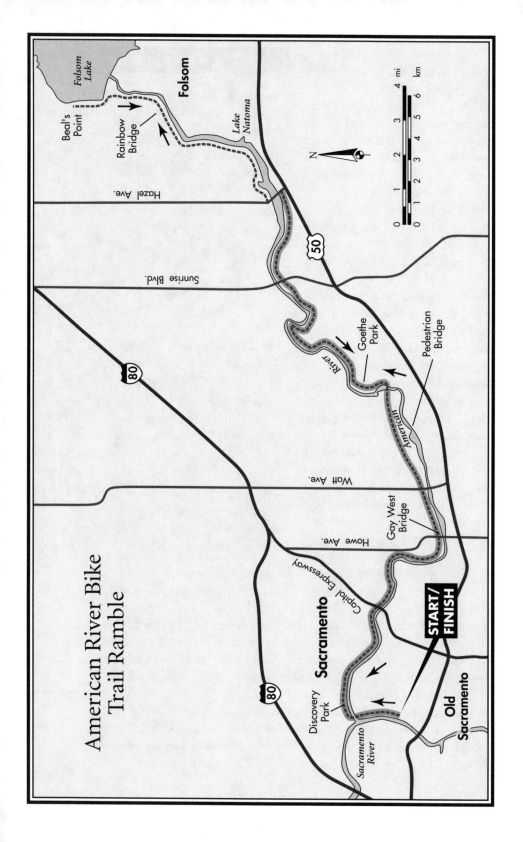

American River Bike
Trail Ramble

0.0 Old Sacramento. Follow the American River Bike Trail north along the Sacramento River.

1.0 Cross the Discovery Park Bridge. Loop to the left underneath the bridge. You are on the bike trail. The painted mileage markers begin here.

3.5 Cross Northgate Boulevard.

8.0 Pass Campus Commons Golf Course.

9.0 Pass the Guy West Bridge. (To return to Old Sacramento directly, cross the bridge, turn right on the levee trail, and follow it to J Street. Take J Street through the underpass, and turn left on Fifty-sixth Street for a block. Turn right on M Street, then right on Thirty-fifth. Left on L Street. Right on Alhambra for a block. Left on K Street. Left on Fourteenth for a block. Right on L. Left on Ninth for a block. Right on Capitol Mall. (This route is known as "Generic" by locals.)

15.0 Goethe Park.

21.0 Fair Oaks Bridge. This is a pedestrian bridge.

24.0 Nimbus Fish Hatchery. Cross the American River on the Hazel Avenue walkway.

29.0 Old Rainbow Bridge at Folsom.

32.0 Beal's Point. To return to Old Sacramento, follow directions in reverse.

Past Fair Oaks the parkway is lined with dredge tailings from the days of hydraulic mining. It then passes the Nimbus Fish Hatchery and crosses the river on the Hazel Avenue Bridge to run along the north side of Lake Natoma, until finally reaching the town of Folsom, another potential place to stop.

After crossing the old Rainbow Bridge at Folsom, the trail finally begins to climb a bit, and the pavement ends at Beal's Point in another 4 miles. On this section riders should stop to admire the beginnings of the American River gorge and to contemplate the massive Folsom Prison on the other side of the river.

One nice thing about the trail is that it is accessible in dozens of places, and several easy rides can be started in Folsom, the Nimbus Hatchery, Fair Oaks, Goethe Park, Sacramento State, or Old Sacramento. The trail is always a great place to take kids and offers them plenty of natural entertainment as well as places to stop and eat.

25

Foresthill Classic

FORESTHILL — MIDDLE FORK OF THE AMERICAN RIVER —
RUBICON RIVER — PLACER BIG TREE GROVE — NORTH FORK
OF THE AMERICAN RIVER — FORESTHILL

E pic *is the best word to describe any ride out of Foresthill, a Sierra community that straddles the Foresthill Divide, between two great canyons of the American River. The Foresthill Classic takes in both these canyons, burying itself in the American Rubicon Gorge and glimpsing the canyon of the American River North Fork. Along the way it includes one of the most beautiful descents and one of the most intensely challenging climbs in the Sierra.*

Cruising the pine-studded Foresthill Road.

Foresthill is a Gold Rush town that is gradually being encroached upon by late twentieth-century civilization (the population has grown to nearly four thousand people). There is a modern grocery there, Worton's, which is a good place to stock up, as this will be the only food source you will see. In summer this can be a four-water-bottle plus CamelBak ride, and since there is only one place to get water after the start and it will be very hot on the climbs, prepare yourself. Once you leave Foresthill you will not pass another house of any kind for more than 50 miles, and there is a lot of tough terrain along the way.

This ride begins with a huge smile. That's because once you turn onto Mosquito Ridge Road, you are descending along the Rubicon/ Middle Fork of the American Gorge on one of the world's most beautiful roads. Even though you are going downhill, you are also going into the mountains, so as you descend, the walls of the gorge rise above you. The scenery is spectacular; just don't spend too much time looking over the edge at the Rubicon, 2,000 feet below.

Another surprise here: Under normal summertime conditions, as you descend, you will notice the temperature growing warmer. Foresthill is at 3,200 feet; the river is at 1,100 or so, and the canyon traps heat. On summer afternoons it is not unusual for the temperature to be more than 100 degrees.

Mosquito Ridge actually doesn't go all the way to the Rubicon but

THE BASICS

Start: Foresthill, 16 miles east of Auburn, on Foresthill Road. Park along Foresthill Road, between the old town and Mosquito Ridge Road.

Length: 63.3 miles.

Terrain: Prolonged descending and climbing. Very hot in summer; snow may block roads into June. Roads are relatively free of traffic and smooth, except for a 5-mile unpaved stretch on Road 43 near Robinson Flat. High-volume, durable tires are recommended, and good off-roading skills are required.

Food: No food on the route. Water only at Big Trees. Worton's Grocery in Foresthill is a good place to stock up before the ride.

For more information: Cambria Bicycle Emporium, 483 Grass Valley Highway, Auburn, CA 95603; (530) 823–2900. Foresthill Ranger Station, 22830 Foresthill Road, Foresthill, CA 95631; (530) 367–2224; www.r5.fs.fed.us/tahoe/ fhrd/tnfforesthill.html.

Maps: DeLorme Northern California Atlas and Gazetteer, map 80; Krebs Cycle Products, Lake Tahoe and Gold Country map.

bottoms out at Peavine Creek (also called the North Fork of the Middle Fork of the American). You'll probably notice a few cars parked along here, as this is a dipping spot for the locals. Afterward an extraordinary 25-mile climb begins.

After passing Ralston Ridge Road, Mosquito Ridge Road climbs steadily up the north side of the divide between the American Middle Fork and Peavine Creek. Traffic here is nonexistent, and the scenery is sublime. On the right are towering cliffs seeping with water, and on the left is a vertical drop to Peavine Creek far below.

After 10 miles the road breaks into the high country and passes the Placer Big Tree Grove, the most northerly grove of the sequoias. This is a good stopping point since it's the only source of water on this route. A tar-and-chip road

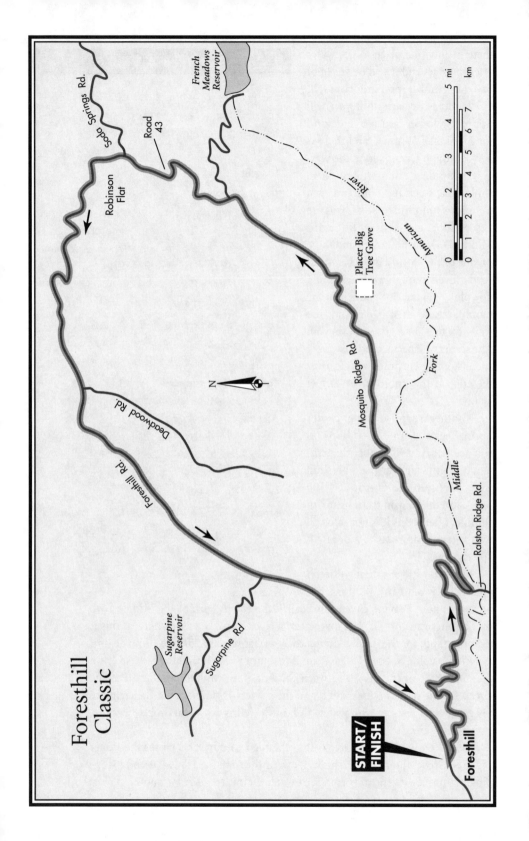

0.0 South on Foresthill Road.

0.3 Left on Mosquito Ridge Road. Two thousand-foot descent over next 11 miles.

12.0 Pass Ralston Cutoff. Continue on Mosquito. Steady climbing for the next 23 miles.

26.0 Placer Big Tree Grove. The only place for water on this route.

29.8 Left toward Robinson Flat on Road 43. Gravel for 5 miles, sometimes steep. (Do *not* go right to French Meadows Reservoir.)

35.5 Left on Foresthill Road. Start downhill.

46.9 Pass Deadwood Road.

54.2 Pass Sugarpine Road.

63.3 Ride ends in Foresthill.

of about 2 miles leads to a parking lot with bathrooms and water. We highly recommend that you refill bottles here and drink up. The only water beyond this point will be in the form of meager creeks and streams, but these are often dangerous and not at all potable even if you use a high-tech filter that can filter out *Giardia*. Check with the Forest Service about water conditions before heading out.

Mosquito Ridge Road is now at a height of more than 5,000 feet, and you will notice a lot of alpine flora, including Douglas fir, ponderosa pine, spruce, and also bear clover, known for its distinctive creosote smell. You may also experience some shortness of breath. The grade at this point is not particularly steep, but you'll soon be on the steep grades and rough gravelly surface of Road 43 heading to Robinson Flat. Only the very strong and determined cyclist will be able to ride this entire stretch without a dismount, but the walking sections are short, and generally the road is quite pleasant. Also, this road is not plowed and often remains snow covered and impassable until June. It's advisable to call the Forest Service to check on road conditions.

Robinson Flat tops out at 6,700 feet at the intersection with Foresthill Road. From here swooshing 20 miles of downhill takes you back to the start. If you wish to soak up a little more of that backwoods ambiance, stop for dinner at the Forest House Restaurant in the center of old Foresthill.

Iowa Hill Challenge

COLFAX — IOWA HILL — FORESTHILL — COLFAX

Got a triple chainring? You may want one for this challenge. Your reward for completing thigh-burning climbs is spectacular views of the American River Canyon. After a strenuous start the route becomes more varied, rambling through historic mining areas, skirting the alpine highlands, and returning through Foresthill and the American River Canyon.

The route starts in the old railroad center of Colfax and abruptly descends 1,000 serpentine feet to the American River before climbing up the edge of the canyon wall. For the first 2 miles, the grade is approximately 15 percent. For long stretches of the climb, the road is barely oxcart wide, so even though you may be creeping along at 4 miles per hour, don't count on being able to zigzag your way up. Unless you have the legs of LeMond and the lungs of Lance Armstrong, expect to stop at least once on the way up.

Iowa Hill tops out into a beautiful, butterfly-filled stream canyon. It then winds along ridges created by hydraulic mining from the Gold Rush days, before reaching the town of Iowa Hill. The general store is a welcome stop.

Continuing on, the road narrows to one lane of chip and tar as it winds through the alpine country of Strawberry Flat to Sugarpine Reservoir. Douglas fir and ponderosa pine are common here. They keep you company in this lonely, remote place.

After Foresthill, Yankee Jim's Road is paved for the first 3 miles then turns to dirt as it winds through American River Ravine. You'll pass some lovely waterfalls on the way down, but keep your eyes on the road—there's quite a drop-off to the right. At the bridge there is a swimming spot popular with

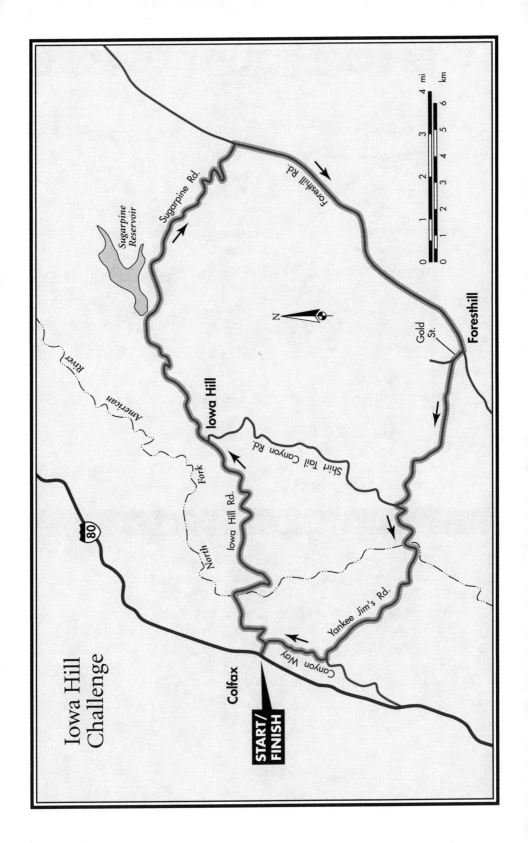

Iowa Hill Challenge

Colfax

Iowa Hill

Foreshill

Sugarpine Reservoir

American River

North Fork

Sugarpine Rd.

Foreshill Rd.

Gold St.

Shirt Tail Canyon Rd.

Iowa Hill Rd.

Yankee Jim's Rd.

Canyon Way

START/FINISH

80

N

4 mi

km

0   1   2   3

0   1   2   3   4   5   6

THE BASICS

Start: Park on Canyon Way, the frontage road on the east side of I-80 in Colfax.

Length: 46.5 miles.

Terrain: Very steep descending and climbing on Iowa Hill. Otherwise rolling. Eroded dirt surface on the descent of Yankee Jim's Road. Cross or mountain bike recommended.

Food: Grocery stores in Iowa Hill and Foresthill. Restaurants in Foresthill and Colfax. Ruby's Cafe on the northeast side of Highway 80 at the Colfax exit is a great eatery.

For more information: Cambria Bicycle Emporium, 483 Grass Valley Highway, Auburn, CA 95603; (530) 823-2900.

Maps: DeLorme *Northern California Atlas and Gazetteer,* maps 79 and 80; Krebs Cycle Products, *Lake Tahoe and Gold Country* map.

locals. The descent is rocky and rough and is best done on a mountain or cross bike. The climb is not hard. Yankee Jim's Road is paved for the last few miles into Colfax.

If you have some energy left upon returning, the old town of Colfax is worth exploring. Once a rail center, Colfax is now a quiet, nontouristy, Victorian hamlet a mile or so off the freeway. There are several good restaurants and a health-food store. It's a nice place to take a walk.

MILES AND DIRECTIONS

0.0 Colfax exit off I-80. Take Canyon Way north following I-80.

0.8 Right on Iowa Hill Road. Steep descent followed by steep climb.

10.7 Town of Iowa Hill. Stay on Iowa Hill Road.

15.7 Sugarpine Reservoir. Iowa Hill Road turns into Sugarpine Road.

23.5 Right on Foresthill Road.

32.4 Right on Gold Street in Foresthill and then veer left onto Yankee Jim's Road. Gravel begins after 3 miles.

45.5 Right on Canyon Way.

46.5 Ride ends in Colfax.

Placerville Classic and Cruise Option

PLACERVILLE — AMERICAN RIVER SOUTH FORK — ELDORADO
NATIONAL FOREST — GEORGETOWN — PLACERVILLE

P*lacerville, formerly known as Old Dry Diggins and Hangtown, is a charming former Gold Rush village in the Sierra foothills just off Highway 50. Historic buildings dating from the nineteenth century dot Main Street, including Pearson's Soda Works, now a coffee shop, at the east end of town. On hot days, and there are many, you can cool off in the old mining tunnel at the back of Pearson's.*

This ride is demanding. But it's scenic and, with the exception of the immediate Placerville area and parts of Highway 193, lightly trafficked, though this may change as more homes are being built in the area. Alpine gearing is recommended, as are strong brakes.

Start the challenge on Main Street in downtown Placerville and head east. Once out of town, the route climbs and then descends along Mosquito Road into a steep canyon drained by the South Fork of the American River. This descent requires prolonged braking on a rough 15-percent grade, so take care. Before you begin your descent, stop and look east for a glimpse of the snow-capped Sierra peaks.

At the bottom of the descent, you'll cross a narrow suspension bridge spanning the rockbound river chasm. A steep, switchback road climbs out, reaching gorgeous upland meadows, where expensive-looking homes have been built in recent years—many are clustered around the air strip at the summit.

Descending into the American River Canyon again on Rock Creek Road, the pavement gets curvy and seems to roll downward forever. Rock Creek bridge, at the bottom of the descent, is a local swimming spot.

The climb out of the canyon is gradual and at times seems almost effortless. Rock Creek Road ends at Highway 193, still a bit above the river. If you don't feel up for the full challenge, turn left on Highway 193 to return to Placerville, which is a screaming descent down to the river and then a slow, steep climb back to town. But if you are feeling particularly chipper and strong and are packing enough water, turn right toward the Eldorado Wilderness.

Here the adventure begins. At the top of the climb on Highway 193, turn off onto tiny Shoofly Road, a real roller coaster of a road through the pines. At Spanish Flat the road crosses a creek valley and then twists into the Eldorado National Forest. Houses become fewer and fewer and eventually disappear. The road at this point is not much wider than a bike trail as it climbs up Darling Ridge to more than 3,000 feet. Ponderosa pines and other alpine flora appear, as do a vast network of dirt trails. Unless you have a lot of time and a very good map, we don't recommend you take any of these. If you get lost, it's rather unlikely that you'll run into anyone to help guide you out.

Following the pavement, however, you eventually come out on Wentworth Springs Road, which leads to Georgetown, a fairly sizable, though isolated, Sierra community. A grocery store and several saloons are available for refreshments.

To return to Placerville simply take Highway 193 south. A roaring but fairly safe descent takes you back down the American River Canyon, past Rock Creek and across the river at Chili Bar. This former town site was situated on a gravel bar on the inside of the river bend. In Gold Rush days such bars were mined for gold, and settlements often formed on them. Chili Bar happened to be populated by Chileans. It has long since been wiped away by countless floods. The climb into Placerville is still there: It's a good thousand feet, with some 10-percent grades.

After this ride you'll probably want to visit one of Placerville's restaurants, perhaps Tortilla Flats for Mexican food or Powell Brothers for wonderful clam chowder and special pan roasts (a seafood stew). You should also check out the Placerville Hardware, said to be the oldest hardware store in the West.

Suspension bridge over the American River South Fork.

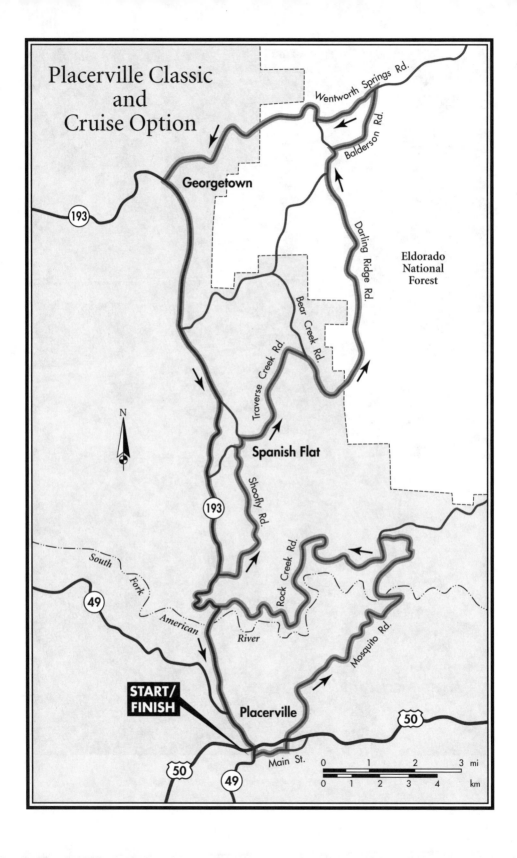

Placerville Classic and Cruise Option

Wentworth Springs Rd.

Balderson Rd.

Georgetown

(193)

Darling Ridge Rd.

Eldorado National Forest

Bear Creek Rd.

Traverse Creek Rd.

N

Spanish Flat

(193)

Shoofly Rd.

Rock Creek Rd.

South Fork

(49)

American

River

Mosquito Rd.

START/ FINISH

Placerville

(50)

(50)

(49)

Main St.

0   1   2   3 mi

0   1   2   3   4 km

0.0 Main Street and Highway 49, Placerville. Go east on Main Street.

1.0 Left on Mosquito Road.

1.5 Begin climbing.

2.6 Summit and bear left to stay on Mosquito Ridge Road (Union Ridge Road continues straight). Begin long descent with brief rollers.

5.7 Cross bridge. Begin climbing.

8.7 Pass Mosquito Cutoff Road on left.

9.4 Left on Rock Creek Road.

14.1 Cross bridge over creek. Begin climbing.

16.0 Summit.

19.8 Right on Highway 193. (For the short loop, go left on Highway 193 and left on Highway 49 in Placerville. Distance to Placerville: 4.2 miles.)

22.2 Right on Shoofly Road. Begin steep climb.

22.8 Summit. Begin rollers.

25.5 Right on Spanish Flat.

25.9 Right on Traverse Creek, called FR 11.

26.7 Cross bridge and begin climb.

28.1 Summit.

28.3 Right on Bear Creek Road/FR 11. This becomes Darling Ridge/FR 11.

29.2 Campground. Begin climbing.

31.0 Summit.

35.2 Right on Balderston Road (unmarked).

37.1 Left on Wentworth Springs Road. Begin descending.

38.2 Begin climbing.

39.1 Summit.

43.2 Georgetown. Left on Highway 193.

54.3 American River crossing at Chili Bar. Begin climbing.

58.8 Summit. Left on Highway 49 toward Placerville.

59.3 Ride ends in Placerville.

Diamond Valley Ramble

WOODFORDS — DIAMOND VALLEY — WOODFORDS

*A*lpine County, located just south of Lake Tahoe, is best known *for the ominously named Markleeville Death Ride. This annual 129-mile gruelathon through the Sierra includes climb after punishing climb, with more than 16,000 feet of elevation in one day. It's the ultimate high-altitude endorphin extravaganza for the super fit (see www.deathride.com). But if you're among those more subtly than super fit, don't go spinning off to other parts just yet. There are also rides on the Sunny Side of Life here in Alpine County, and this 11.2-mile ramble is one of them.*

Leaving from Woodfords, the ride starts with a short, steep pitch of road as you climb up Highway 89 to the turnoff at Diamond Valley Road. Once your wheels hit this thin ribbon of asphalt, all cars disappear and the quiet country-side takes over. Get about 1 mile away from Highway 89 and you are utterly alone. There are no campgrounds, no homes, not even an abandoned shack. The scenery alternates from pastoral meadows to the scrubby bushes and barren hills of high desert, with the sylvan, snow-covered peaks of the Sierra Nevada as a backdrop. It all feels very Old West in a Hollywood kind of way. You almost expect to see a pair of dust-covered cowboys loping through the sagebrush on their horses.

But reality returns as you come across the Hung-a-Lel-Ti, a southern band of the Washoe tribe of California-Nevada, at mile 5.2. These are not the Native Americans of Hollywood movies. The barren patch of land that they call home is all that the government has allowed. And there are no tepees, no horses, only modest residences and broken-down cars.

Start: Intersection of Highway 88 and Highway 89 in Woodfords.

Length: 11.2 miles.

Terrain: Mostly flat; some rolling hills; virtually carless roads.

Food: General store in Woodfords; no food available on ride.

For more information: Alpine County Chamber of Commerce, P.O. Box 265, Markleeville, CA 96120; (530) 694–2475. Big Daddy's Bikes, 1546 Highway 395, Gardnerville, NV 89410; (775) 782–7077.

Maps: DeLorme *Northern California Atlas and Gazetteer*, map 90; Compass Maps, *Alpine, Amador, and Sacramento Counties*.

As Diamond Valley Road curls around this small reservation, you can deviate from the prescribed ride by taking Long Valley Road (which becomes Indian Creek Road when you cross the Nevada state line) all the way to the larger Washoe reservation in Dresslerville. From there you can hook up with busy Highway 395, which intersects with Highway 88 in Minden and heads back to Woodfords.

Continuing past the reservation, you turn left onto Carson River Road, just before Highway 88. The road ambles through the Carson River Valley, delivering you all the way back to Woodfords. There you can pick up a snack at the general store and smile for having taken a ride on the sunny side of life.

MILES AND DIRECTIONS

0 From the intersection of Highway 88 and Highway 89 in Woodfords, turn right onto Highway 89 toward Markleeville.

5 Left onto Diamond Valley Road.

2 Hung-a-Lel-Ti, southern band of the Washoe tribe of California and Nevada.

4 Left onto Carson River Road.

5 Left onto Highway 88.

9 Woodfords city limits.

2 Ride ends at junction of Highway 88 and Highway 89.

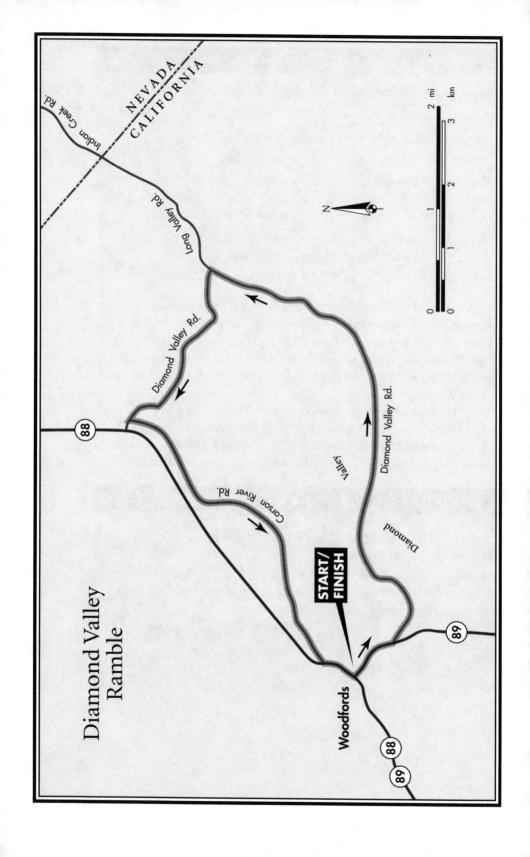

Diamond Valley
Ramble

June Lake Loop Ramble

JUNE LAKE — SILVER LAKE — GRANT LAKE — MONO LAKE

J ust above the briny but beautiful aura of Mono Lake lies a verdant and lush quaternity of emerald lakes set in alpine granite. June, Silver, Gull, and Grant are their names, and they are a burst of life on the edge of the high desert. The June Lake Loop Ramble threads the four together by way of a small string of a road on the edge of the Ansel Adams Wilderness. During the winter months the road and surrounding area sleep beneath unplowed snow, but in summer the road clears, the cabins reopen, and vacationers return to float on rafts and light up barbecues. Yet while it is well used, the area is not overused and remains a dreamy place where the atmosphere is pleasant and the living good.

Traveling by two wheels is a great way to experience this little corner of the eastern Sierra. The ride begins at the junction of Highways 395 and 158 (June Lake Junction) and immediately climbs up the charmingly named Oh! Ridge before dropping into the resort town of June Lake. From here the terrain presents few challenges as the road skims the shores of each lake. Keep in mind, however, that the altitude hovers around 7,500 feet, so even though there aren't any major climbs, you may nevertheless get a wind-out-of-the–sails feeling whenever the road gently rises up to greet you.

Along with being thin, the air can also be brisk, particularly in the more shaded sections. This changes near Grant Lake, where the sun beats down a little

Start: June Lake Junction at southern end of June Lake Loop Road. (Highway 158).

Length: 23.2 or 34.6 miles.

Terrain: Mostly flat with some rolling hills. Two moderate climbs and a descent. Less traffic on Highway 158; heavier traffic on Highway 395.

Food: There's a general store/gas station at the ride start, plus restaurants and stores in June Lake—Trout Town Joe is a good spot for a smoothie.

For more information: Inyo National Forest Mammoth Lakes Visitors Center; (760) 924–5500. Mammoth Lakes Ranger Station, P.O. Box 148, Mammoth Lake, CA 93546; (760) 934–2505.

Maps: DeLorme *Northern California Atlas and Gazetteer*, map 112.

harder and the temperature rises with the descent. This is also where the alpine lushness fades, and the desert sage and juniper return.

After 17 miles on the loop road, you'll be faced with a decision. You can either turn about-face and retrace the peaceful path back to June Lake Junction or turn right onto the more trafficked Highway 395, the main artery to nearby Mammoth Lakes and points beyond, and follow it for 6 miles. Either way there's some moderate climbing involved.

There's also a 10-mile spur option off the main loop. A half mile down Highway 395 is the turnoff for Mono Lake and its extraordinary tufa towers (the towers are located 5 miles from the turnoff). These odd structures, formed by natural mineral deposits,

Mono Lake's mysterious tufa towers.

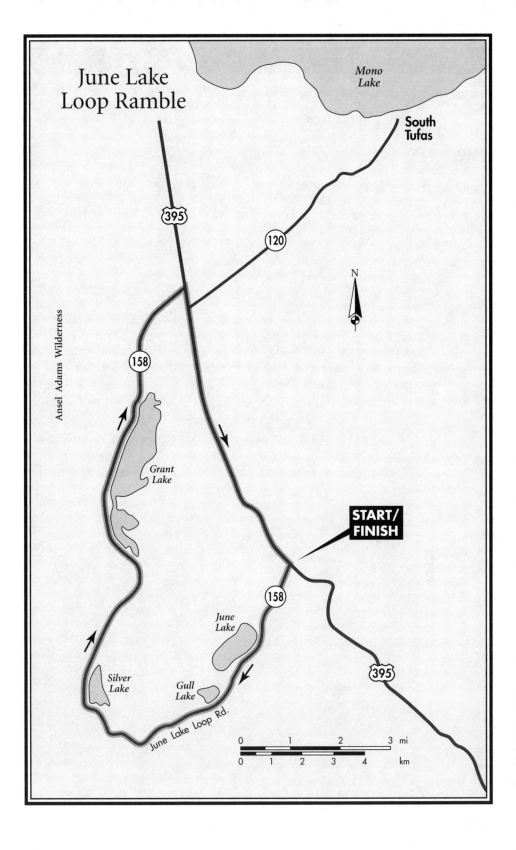

June Lake
Loop Ramble

Mono
Lake

South
Tufas

395

120

N

158

Ansel Adams Wilderness

Grant
Lake

START/
FINISH

158

June
Lake

Silver
Lake

Gull
Lake

395

June Lake Loop Rd.

0   1   2   3 mi
0   1   2   3   4 km

MILES AND DIRECTIONS

0.0 Take Highway 158 (June Lake Loop Road) toward June Lake.

0.7 Begin climb.

1.1 Oh! Ridge.

2.4 June Lake.

3.4 Gull Lake.

6.5 Silver Lake. Begin long descent.

11.1 Grant Lake.

17.3 Right onto Highway 395. (Option: You can turn around at the intersection and retrace your path on Highway 158 for a total of 34.6 miles.)

17.9 Mono Lake, South Tufa turnoff option (will add 10 miles to total).

18.9 Begin gradual climb back to June Lake Junction.

23.2 Ride ends at intersection of Highway 395 and Highway 158.

were exposed as water flowing from the eastern Sierra was diverted to Los Angeles. As the lake level dropped, the towers slowly emerged. But today the towers are again slowly slipping back into their watery world. After years of protests against the diversions, water is again flowing into Mono. In sum, the lake is worth a visit—the best times are at sunrise and sunset.

If you're looking for more action and are feeling energetic, there's plenty more in the area to explore. If you brought your fat-tire bike along, you're in luck, as the area offers some of the best mountain-biking terrain in the state.

North Coast
and Mountains

Lost Coast Classic

FERNDALE — SCOTIA — AVENUE OF THE GIANTS —
HONEYDEW — PETROLIA — LOST COAST — FERNDALE

anging precipitously on the edge of California, the Lost Coast is like a chaste beauty living in an ivory tower. Despite its eye-popping splendor, the inaccessibility of the land locks it into virtual isolation. When Highway 101 turns inward at Legget, it takes with it the majority of auto-propelled tourists. Only the most intrepid of travelers, the ones who can handle not having a major highway or city anywhere nearby, make it to the isolated shores of the Lost Coast. Because of this, the area is ideal for cycling. The secluded backroads that make up this ride range from dense, dark redwood groves to a jagged coastline of black-sand beaches stretching out to meet the Pacific Ocean.

The ride takes you almost 75 miles before your wheels actually roll along the Lost Coast. For the sake of convenience, the ride starts at an accessible locale and gets progressively "lost" with every mile. The Victorian hamlet of Ferndale is the starting point for the ride. Renowned for its "butterfat" mansions, the town was built by well-to-do dairymen during the town's nineteenth-century heyday. The abundance of historic architecture, which includes Queen Anne, Eastlake, and Classical Revival, has caused the entire village to be dubbed a State Historical Landmark. This ornamental charm stands in ultimate contrast to the unrestrained beauty of the Lost Coast.

This route is patterned after the annual Unknown Coast Weekend century ride, organized by the Chico Velo Cycling Club and considered one of California's toughest centuries. And after 8 miles of cycling, you'll get a taste of what you're in for when you encounter your first big hill en route to Rio Dell. Scotia, a town almost completely owned by the Pacific Lumber Company, is

Ferndale viewed on the way down "the Wildcat."

only a short ride away. Somewhere in the hills overlooking this town stands Luna, the redwood made famous by activist Julia Butterfly Hill, who lived in the tree for two years.

THE BASICS

Start: Intersection of Ocean Street and Main Street in downtown Ferndale.

Length: 100 miles.

Terrain: Three extended climbs, many rolling hills, heavy winds with gusts of sand on coast. Weekend and tourist traffic on Avenue of the Giants. Temperatures can vary dramatically, so dress in layers.

Food: You can get a good breakfast in Ferndale, right on Main Street. There are stores in Honeydew and Petrolia where you can buy some snacks for lunch and stock up on food to carry you through the day. Back in Ferndale treat yourself to a heaping big meal.

For more information: Henderson Center Bicycle, 2811 F Street, Eureka, CA 95501; (707) 443-9861.

Maps: DeLorme *Northern California Atlas and Gazetteer*, maps 42 and 52; Krebs Cycle Products, *California North Coast* map.

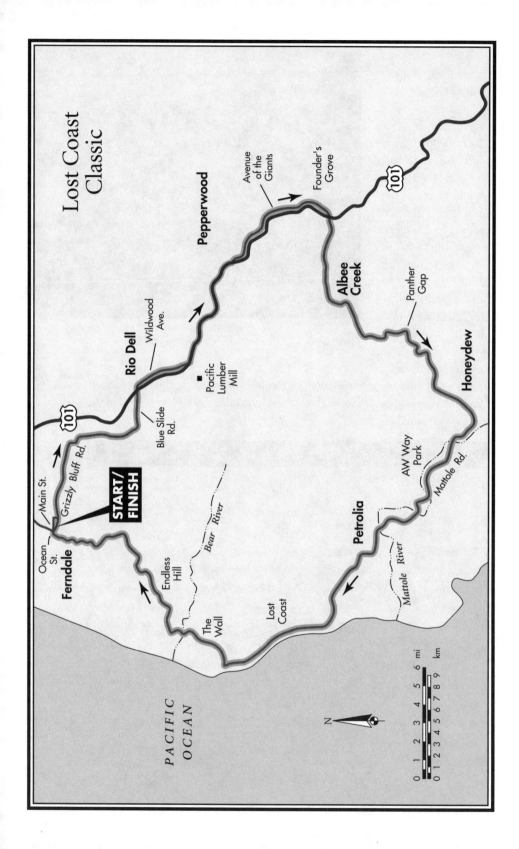

0.0 South on Ocean Street at the intersection of Ocean and Main in Ferndale.

3.7 Straight past Waddington Road; Ocean Street becomes Grizzly Bluff Road.

5.4 Pass Grizzly Bluff School.

13.1 Grizzly Bluff Road becomes Blue Slide Road; descend into Rio Dell. Right onto Wildwood Avenue.

14.4 Scotia. Pass Pacific Lumber Mill.

15.9 Enter Highway 101S. Yes, this is a legal bike route!

21.7 Exit Highway 101 at Pepperwood. Left at stop sign onto Avenue of the Giants.

31.7 Right onto Mattole Road toward Bull Creek, passing under 101. (If you enter Weott, you've missed the turn.)

38.0 Albee Creek.

46.7 Begin ascent of Panther Gap.

48.3 Summit. Be careful on the twisty descent.

53.0 Honeydew. Right to stay on Mattole Road.

63.0 AW Way Park, a county campground.

69.0 Petrolia. Stay on paved road through town.

73.0 Lost Coast.

81.5 Begin ascent of The Wall; 18-percent grade.

82.5 Summit. Descend to the Bear River.

86.7 Begin climb of the Endless Hill.

96.0 Summit. Begin yet another steep, winding descent.

100.0 Sharp right at bottom of Wildcat Grade. Ride ends at Ocean and Main Streets in Ferndale.

The PLC lumber empire extends from one end of town to the other, and when you finally roll to the end of it, you'll turn onto Highway 101 south. As you pedal onto the ramp, your ability to measure your progress in small chunks from city to city all but disappears. After nearly 6 miles you'll leave the rush of cars behind and greet the ancient redwoods as you pedal onto the famed Avenue of the Giants. The soft, dank shelter of these towering trees yields a mossy carpet of forest floor, with mushrooms sprouting everywhere in a wild frenzy.

A good side trip at this point is to visit Founder's Grove, which is 300 yards beyond the turnoff for Bull Creek Road. The Dyerville Giant, once the world's tallest tree, but now fallen, is worth a visit.

Your route tumbles deeper into the secluded world of nature as you turn onto Bull Creek Road and begin a gentle, quiet climb through the redwoods. The road is a pastoral poem where sheep roam freely, often holding court right

The classic charm of downtown Ferndale.

in the middle of the road. When you reach the tiny town of Honeydew, at mile 55.6, you'll find a store where you can refuel and chill out for a while. From here country roads transport you through the town of Petrolia, which also has a store, and finally deposit you at the Lost Coast. Here, at mile 73, much hardship awaits.

At the coast, particularly in the afternoon, gusty winds laced with sand can drop your cruising speed down to less than 10 mph. Cattle wandering aimlessly along the road provide that obstacle-course element so often missing in other rides. And then there's The Wall. At mile 81.5 your windbeaten limbs will be forced to attack a 1-mile, 18-percent grade. And right after you've recovered from that, you'll be faced with the Endless Hill, thrown in for good measure at mile 86.7, just to ensure that you've really worked for your 100 miles. After 85 miles of pedaling, a bump on the road can seem endless—and this 8-mile climb ain't no bump.

Just remember, when you reach the summit, you're finally home free. A swooshing, spiraling descent down a curving slope, locally known as "The Wildcat," drops you back into Ferndale and leaves you finishing the ride with the perfect combination of feelings: accomplishment for riding 100 miles and exhilaration for getting to end them with a thrilling descent.

Dyerville Loop Cruise

FOUNDERS' GROVE — DYERVILLE LOOP ROAD —
HUMBOLDT REDWOODS STATE PARK — AVENUE OF THE
GIANTS — MYERS FLAT — WEOTT — FOUNDERS' GROVE

*I*t is said that the legendary Bigfoot has been routinely spotted in
the wilds of Humboldt County. And on your bike, alone, in the
solitude of an untamed forest, it's easy to shelve your sensibility and
embrace a world where fairies, gnomes, and even sasquatches roam
freely, ready to pop out from around the next corner.

Indeed, the setting is such that anything seems possible on the Dyerville
Loop Cruise. Ancestral redwoods stand stoic at the ride's start, gently whisper-
ing their secrets. Coming out of the cathedral-like woodlands, the Eel River
glistens in its rocky bed, and bunches of blackberries hang heavy along the
roadside in summer. As you begin climbing, all is eerily quiet, except for your
own rhythmic breathing and the rustling of leaves in a passing breeze.

Although this loop ride is only 23 miles, the climbs make it almost a challenge. The roads are steep and rough for the first 9 miles, and the steepest and
longest of the many climbs charges up a wildly pitched dirt-and-gravel fire
road. This steep road requires low gearing, muscle, and technical skill to main-
tain traction. The switchbacks and numerous false summits will do their best
to defeat even the most intrepid of road bikers. High-volume tires are a must
or, better yet, a well-equipped mountain or cross bike.

As you near the summit of the climb, the grade mellows a bit. With your
nose off the proverbial grindstone, wipe the sweat from your brow and see
where your legs and lungs have brought you. Beyond the dense trees that form
a cool canopy above, you may catch glimpses of far-off, snow-covered peaks, as

Start: Founders' Grove, on the Avenue of the Giants, in Humboldt Redwoods State Park.

Length: 23 miles.

Terrain: Steep, extended climbing. Rough roads; 2.2 miles of climbing on dirt and gravel road. Little to no traffic on Dyerville Loop Road and Elk Creek Road; weekend and tourist traffic on Avenue of the Giants. Mountain bikes are recommended due to the steep, dirt climb, but it is possible to complete on a properly equipped (and ridden) road bike.

Food: Two diners and a general store are located in Myers Flat.

For more information: Humboldt Redwoods State Park, P.O. Box 100, Weott, CA 95571; (707) 946-2409.

Maps: DeLorme *Northern California Atlas and Gazetteer,* maps 52 and 53; Krebs Cycle Products, *California North Coast* map.

Bigfoot gears up along the Avenue of the Giants.

well as the Eel River, tiny now and far below. There are no stores, no gas stations, no schools.

Yes, you are in the middle of nowhere. But only 5 miles away is the security of organized nature at Humboldt Redwoods State Park and the famed Avenue of the Giants. As you drop down Elk Creek Road back to the park, notice the dramatic terrain change from rolling, hilltop pastures to the lush valley of the redwood groves.

The flat terrain of the Avenue of the Giants is a gorgeous reprieve from the steep grades of Dyerville Loop and Elk Creek Roads. The avenue, however, gets its share of traffic, particularly herds of Winnebagos that behave as if they own the road. On your bike you can easily make impromptu stops on the Avenue of the Giants to enjoy the dank, dark redwood groves. You also

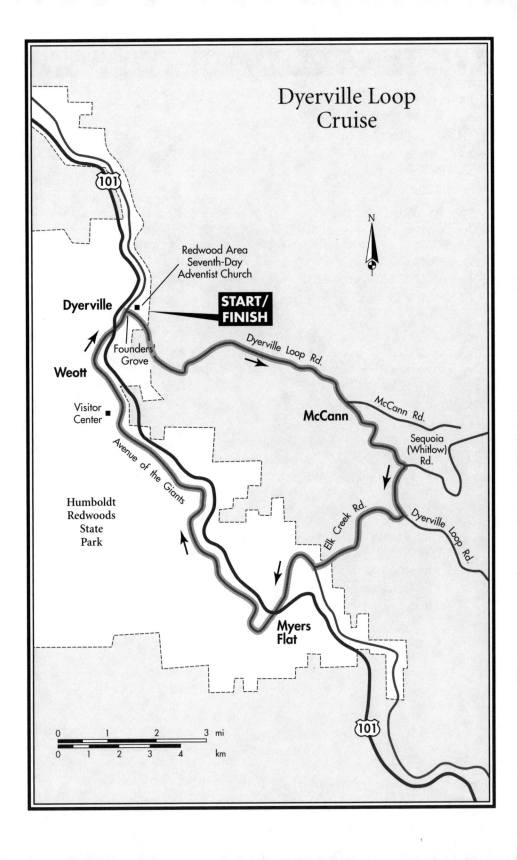

Dyerville Loop
Cruise

N

Redwood Area
Seventh-Day
Adventist Church

Dyerville

**START/
FINISH**

Founders'
Grove

Dyerville Loop Rd.

Weott

McCann Rd.

Visitor
Center

McCann

Sequoia
(Whitlow)
Rd.

Avenue of the Giants

Humboldt
Redwoods
State
Park

Elk Creek Rd.

Dyerville Loop Rd.

**Myers
Flat**

101

0   1   2   3 mi
0   1   2   3   4 km

0.0 East, or left, onto Dyerville Loop Road from Founders' Grove parking lot.

0.6 Leave Humboldt Redwoods State Park.

0.9 Begin climb.

1.7 Summit.

2.4 Ride under subway; pass Redwood Area Seventh-Day Adventist Church. Begin flats.

4.0 Cross railroad track; begin climb.

4.5 Summit. Views of Eel River. Rough road and beginning of rollers.

6.5 McCann Ferry parking lot; veer right on Dyerville Loop Road, which turns to dirt temporarily.

6.8 Pass McCann Road on left, continue straight on Dyerville Loop Road.

7.0 Cross railroad track. Dyerville Loop Road turns to dirt. Begin steep climb. This dirt road is generally in good shape, though the climb can be slippery and traction difficult.

9.2 Summit at Sequoia (Whitlow) Road. Begin descent. Follow sign right to Highway 101.

10.4 Right onto Elk Creek Road. Follow sign that says HIGHWAY 101 5 MILES.

13.2 Right onto Avenue of the Giants at the stop sign. Bottom of descent.

14.6 Myers Flat.

19.4 Humboldt Redwoods State Park visitor center.

20.4 Weott (note 33-foot-high watermark from 1964 flood).

23.6 Right into Founders' Grove. Ride ends at parking lot.

can drop in on the small but impressive visitor center, check out the eccentric locals, stop for a snack in Myers Flat, or just head back to the ride's start and finish at Founders' Grove. Here you can peel off your biking shoes, don your hiking boots, and take a short and easy hike on the Founders' Grove nature trail to stretch out your legs and soak up the wonder of the natural world.

Comptche Cruise

MENDOCINO — LITTLE RIVER — VAN DAMME STATE PARK —
PYGMY FOREST — COMPTCHE — MENDOCINO

H ighway 1 curls groggily into the misty oceanside town of
Mendocino. From the distance the town looks tiny and
sleepy as it juts out on a rocky, jagged edge to meet the Pacific Ocean. A
closer inspection, however, reveals a lot of tourist-driven cheesiness
behind the town's charming New England facade. Yet despite its
unabashed trendy commercialism, Mendocino (sometimes known as
Spendocino) is, dare I say, cute. But where do you draw the line between
cuteness and gaudiness? How long can you shop? How many driftwood
clocks and paintings of whales can you look at?

This, of course, is
why you have a bike. The
magic of Mendocino lies
outside its city limits and
simply cannot be properly
appreciated or explored
within the confines of an
automobile. From its
rocky coast to its densely
forested inland moun-
tains, Mendocino County
is dramatically beautiful,
with quiet country roads
leading to middle-of-

Mendocino stirs in the morning light.

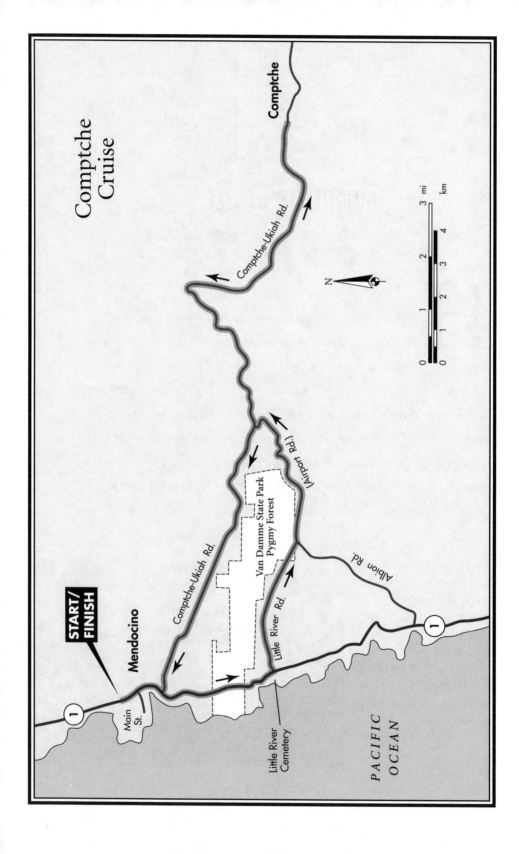

Comptche Cruise

START/FINISH

Mendocino

Main St.

Comptche-Ukiah Rd.

Comptche-Ukiah Rd.

Comptche

Van Damme State Park
Pygmy Forest

(Airport Rd.)

Little River Rd.

Albion Rd.

Little River
Cemetery

PACIFIC
OCEAN

N

0   1   2   3 mi

0   1   2   3   4 km

nowhere towns that seem lost in time.

The Comptche Cruise begins by exiting historic (hysteric?) downtown Mendocino and heading south on the twisty, turny, drop-off-the-face-of-the-earth Highway 1. After 3 miles of riding past oceanside resorts and B&Bs, you'll hit the unassuming Little River Road. This is the kind of road that immediately makes your lips curl upward, because you know, just by looking at the arching trees above it and the way it rambles off to nowhere special, that you've found a killer backroad, the kind of road that cyclists love and drivers hate.

After less than 3 miles on Little River Road, you'll come to the Van Damme State Park Pygmy Forest, a place that lives up to its intriguing name and is well worth a quick look. A raised wooden walkway twists and turns in a maniacal maze through decades-old trees that stand no taller than 4 feet because of the highly acidic soil content and poor drainage.

THE BASICS

Start: Mendocino, at the intersection of Main Street and Highway 1.

Length: 32.9 miles.

Terrain: One major climb, some rollers, lengthy flat stretches on quiet backroads.

Food: Health-food market and a variety of restaurants in Mendocino; one small store in Comptche.

For more information: Catch a Canoe & Bicycles, Too! at The Stanford Inn by the Sea, Highway 1 at Comptche-Ukiah Road, Mendocino; (707) 937–0273; www.stanfordinn. com/canoes.html. Bicycle rentals available.

Note: The Mendocino Coast is an area where you may want to bring your mountain bike. Nearby Jackson State Forest has abundant trails and is open to bicycles.

Maps: DeLorme *Northern California Atlas and Gazetteer,* map 73; Krebs Cycle Products, *California North Coast* map.

At the end of Little River Road, which changes to Airport Road, you reach the beginning of Comptche-Ukiah Road. There may be no sign to tell you what road you're on or where it leads to, but turn right and you'll be heading for Comptche, which is another 9 miles of near-orgasmic cycling away. The Comptche-Ukiah Road is cut into the side of a mountain with a severe drop-off to the redwood valleys far below it. To the left your backdrop is an unending horizon of tree-covered mountains, dreamily softened by the fog that often hovers at their tops. To the right a lush wall of damp, thick forest hugs the side of the road.

After you have cycled only a few miles on this glorious road's summit, the route swoops downward to Comptche. Four miles of descending carries you out of the forested woodlands and into the open grasslands, complete with small farms and houses, lazy cows, and sheep. From here 5 relatively flat miles lead you to the booming metropolis of Comptche, featuring one post office, one store with gas station, one church, and one school. Stop for a snack at the market and relax with the Comptche locals, who can often be found hanging

0.0 Right onto Highway 1 at the intersection of Highway 1 and Main Street in Mendocino. Traffic here is usually heavy during tourist season. Exercise caution as you cross over the Big River Bridge.

2.5 Pass entrance to Van Damme State Park.

3.1 Left onto Little River/Airport Road, immediately past Little River Cemetery.

5.8 Van Damme State Park Pygmy Forest to the left, Albion Road to the right. Continue straight on Little River Road.

9.0 Little River Road comes to a **T** at an unmarked road, which is Comptche-Ukiah Road. Turn right. Traffic on Comptche-Ukiah is fairly light, though there are occasional logging trucks.

18.0 Comptche. Turnaround point.

26.1 Intersect with Little River Road; continue straight on Comptche-Ukiah Road.

32.3 Comptche-Ukiah Road comes to a **T** at Highway 1. Turn right.

32.9 Ride ends at intersection of Highway 1 and Main Street in Mendocino.

out on the one bench in front of the one store. (Incidentally, the Comptche-Ukiah Road is now paved all the way to Ukiah, an additional 70 miles round-trip.)

Comptche is a turnaround point, so fuel up for the extended climb back on Comptche-Ukiah Road. This long, gradual ascent provides the same forested vistas but from an opposite, and much slower, perspective. When you get to Little River Road, continue straight on Comptche-Ukiah for a fast and easy descent offering awe-inspiring views of the Pacific Ocean and Mendocino. It's a great payback for all the climbing and a perfect way to end a ride.

Back on Highway 1 you're less than 1 mile away from Mendocino. And after a hearty day of backroads cycling, it's easier to justify your inherent American urge to indulge in the consumer orgy—so get off your bike, visit town, and eat, drink, and shop to your heart's content.

The Mendocino coastline.

33

Patrick's Point Cruise

ARCATA — CLAM BEACH COUNTY PARK —
TRINIDAD — PATRICK'S POINT — ARCATA

O*n a gray day in the North Coast town of Arcata, when the chill seeps to your bones, riding a bike may seem as appealing as skinny-dipping in the Arctic Circle. But not so to local cyclists, who have learned to recognize and appreciate the fog's many nuances, from the mere hovering dampness to the occasional wind-driven scourge. You'll see them clad in waterproof gear with full fenders on their bikes. And if you're able to muster up enough willpower to pull yourself away from your steaming coffee and join them, you'll realize they aren't just enduring the weather; they're actually enjoying it.*

The Patrick's Point Cruise is a favorite local out-and-back ride, which provides dramatic views of the jagged North Coast, on roads mostly free of the dreaded exhaust-spewing beast. The ride starts at Wildberries Marketplace, 13th and G Streets, in downtown Arcata, a gently accepting type of town where the macrobiotic-diet crowd (intelligentsia from Humboldt State University) mixes easily with the meat-and-potatoes crowd (farming and lumber-industry families who've lived here all their lives). Two miles out of Arcata, the pancake-flat road quickly turns rural. The easy curves of Mad River Road lead to the river of the same name, where a narrow arched bike and pedestrian bridge marks the start of the Hammond Bike Path, a well-traveled throughway that takes you through Hiller Park.

The bike path ends in a new residential area, and the route then skirts the Arcata Airport before returning to the coast at Clam Beach County Park and Little River State Beach, where you can ride alongside sandy dunes. (If the wind

THE BASICS

Start: Wildberries Marketplace, Thirteenth and G Streets in downtown Arcata.

Length: 46.8 miles.

Terrain: Mostly flat, with a few rolling hills and one extended climb; 3 miles of moderately trafficked highway riding.

Food: Best bet for food is Arcata. Wildberries is a good source for healthful snacks you can pack in your jersey for the ride. Roger's Market is located six miles into the ride at the intersection of School Road. Also, you can purchase picnic foods and deli sandwiches at the large grocery store in Trinidad.

For more information: Henderson Center Bike Shop, 2811 F Street, Eureka, CA 95501; (701) 443-7827. Life Cycle Bicycles, Fifteenth and G Streets, Arcata, CA 95521; (707) 822-7755.

Maps: DeLorme *Northern California Atlas and Gazetteer,* maps 42 and 32; Krebs Cycle Products, *California North Coast* map.

Packing out of Trinidad Bay.

has been severe, you may find that some of the dunes have crept onto the road.) At the end of the beach road, you'll have approximately 1.5 miles on Highway 101 (an excellent shoulder and perfectly legal), which is also where you'll haul yourself up the ride's only extended climb (less than 0.5 mile) to the Westhaven Drive exit.

From here the slight Scenic Drive winds bold and treacherous above the Pacific, clinging to the edge of a rocky cliff. For motorists it may be a white-knuckle drive, but for cyclists it's cathartic (though quite bumpy at times). The road turns into Patrick's Point Road at the town of Trinidad, which is known for its spectacular bay and lighthouse surrounded by craggy hills. Patrick's Point Road is smoother and faster than Scenic Drive, and before you know it you'll be at the park entrance. But it's another mile into the park to the geographic Patrick's Point, which stands more than 200 feet above the ocean and provides unsurpassed views of the rocky, misty, stoically beautiful North Coast.

Though the coast is a gorgeous sight, the cold air may soon convince you to get back on your bike. From the park just reverse directions and head back in the opposite way toward Arcata. Your return trip may be aided if you think beer. When the ride ends in Arcata, you'll be less than 0.5 mile from the center of town, where a hearty microbrewed beer awaits at the award-winning Humboldt Brewery.

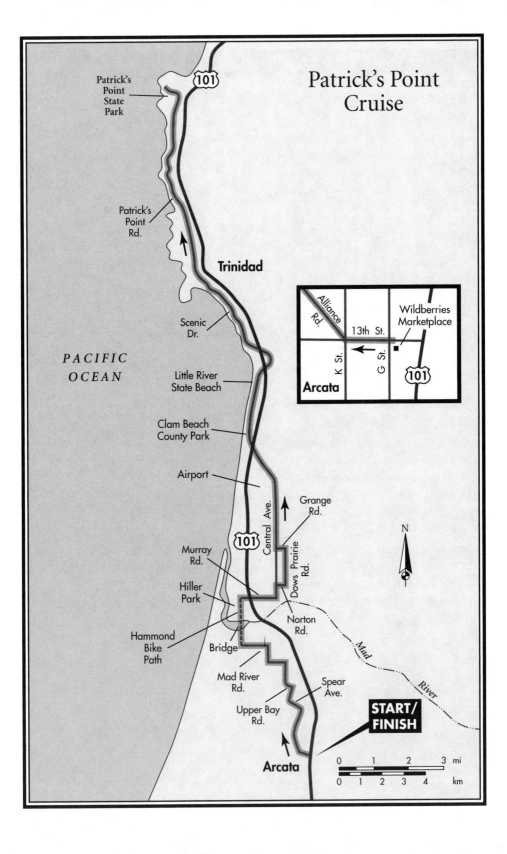

Patrick's Point
Cruise

Patrick's
Point
State
Park

101

Patrick's
Point
Rd.

Trinidad

Scenic
Dr.

*PACIFIC
OCEAN*

Little River
State Beach

Clam Beach
County Park

Airport

Grange
Rd.

Central Ave.

101

Murray
Rd.

Dows Prairie Rd.

Hiller
Park

Norton
Rd.

Hammond
Bike
Path

Bridge

Mad River
Rd.

Spear
Ave.

Upper Bay
Rd.

N

START/
FINISH

Arcata

Alliance
Rd.

13th St.

Wildberries
Marketplace

K St.

G St.

101

Arcata

Mad

River

0   1   2   3 mi

0 1 2 3 4   km

0.0 Left (west) onto 13th Street from Wildberries Market.

0.2 Right at stop sign at bottom of hill onto unmarked Alliance Road.

1.5 Left onto Spear Avenue (beware opening doors on bike lanes).

2.1 Left onto Upper Bay Road across from Pacific Union School.

2.8 Right onto Mad River Road.

5.3 Right onto bike/pedestrian bridge marked COASTAL ACCESS HAMMOND TRAIL/COASTAL TRAIL. The trail is covered in layers of hardened cowpie just beyond the bridge, where cows regularly exit the nearby field.

6.1 Continue straight at Fisher Road/School Road intersection (near Roger's Market). As School Road bends right, continue straight on Fisher Avenue to stay on Hammond Trail (residential area).

6.4 Veer right when Fisher Road turns to dirt to stay on paved bike route.

6.7 Entrance to Hiller Park. Stay right on paved trail.

7.8 Veer sharply right on paved trail (dirt trail continues ahead).

7.9 Trail ends. Continue straight on (unmarked) Murray Road up slight hill (Pacific Sunset housing development on left).

8.2 Cross over Highway 101.

9.0 Left onto Central Avenue.

9.6 Right onto Norton Road.

9.8 Left onto Dows Prarie Road.

10.8 Left onto Grange Road.

11.0 Right onto Central Avenue.

11.9 Cross under Highway 101 and veer right, passing Clam Beach County Park and Little River State Beach.

13.3 Cross 101 overpass. Left on Highway 101 N.

14.3 Begin climb.

14.7 Exit at Westhaven Drive. Summit. Left toward Moonstone Beach at end of exit ramp, then right onto Scenic Drive along coast. The road is rough here, and there may be a few short dirt sections, resulting from landslides over the winter. The terrain is rolling.

17.9 Trinidad. Scenic Drive becomes Patrick's Point Road.

23.4 Patrick's Point State Park. Turnaround point.

Return following the same route. *Note:* Enter Highway 101 S from Scenic Drive after passing Westhaven Drive. Exit Highway 101 S at Little River State Beach (by the weigh station). Also, in Arcata turn onto Twelfth Street from Alliance Avenue to return to Wildberries Marketplace.

Trinity Alps Challenge

WEAVERVILLE — WHISKEYTOWN-SHASTA-TRINITY
NATIONAL RECREATION AREA — TRINITY LAKE —
LEWISTON LAKE — LEWISTON — WEAVERVILLE

At the center of Trinity County's 3,220 square miles of tumbling rivers, massive peaks, turquoise lakes, and protected wilderness is Weaverville, a rustic outpost that proudly recalls its pioneer past. The town's wooden sidewalks and balconies give it an Old West feel; one look around and you can't help but sense the former rough-and-tumble lifestyle of the gold seekers.

But get on your bike and pedal just a few miles away and another history unfolds. The Trinity Alps—ancestral predecessors to Weaverville, mining, and humankind—have their own stories to tell. And spinning up the side of their slopes is the best way to learn what these mountains have to teach.

The Trinity Alps Challenge winds through Trinity National Forest and the Whiskeytown-Shasta-Trinity National Recreation Area, where one climb leads to another as you rise high above aquamarine Clair Engle Lake, a labyrinth of fingered coves formed by Trinity Dam. Though its name suggests a grand thoroughfare, Trinity Dam Boulevard is narrow and remote, with stoic peaks looking down on it with all the power and precariousness of giants. The road can turn rough here, depending on how snowy the last winter was and how recently the county laid down a fresh coat of tar and gravel. After several miles of zigzagging up "the boulevard" to Buckeye Ridge, your climbing pays off in the form of a straight and seemingly endless descent. But what goes down must go up on this ride, and soon you're again spinning uphill in a low gear.

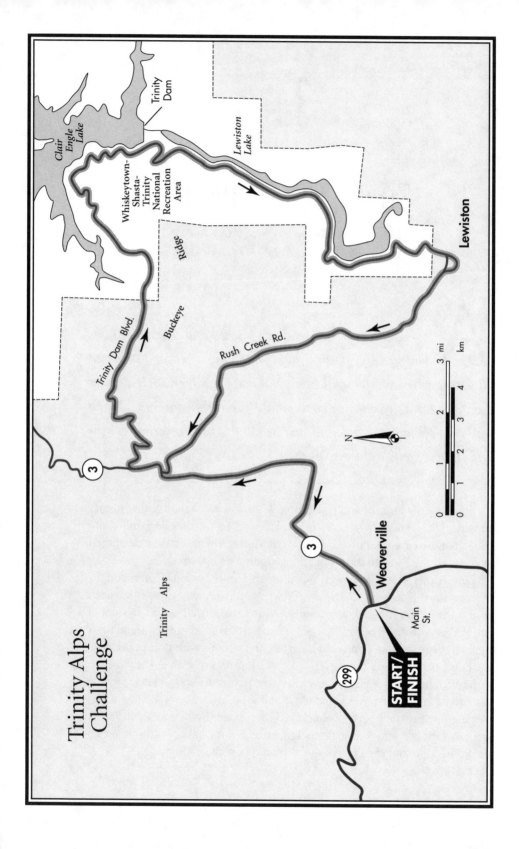

Trinity Alps
Challenge

Start: Intersection of Highway 299 and Highway 3 in downtown Weaverville.

Length: 44.8 miles.

Terrain: Mountain roads, many extended climbs, few flat sections; narrow roads with light to moderate traffic, but watch for RVs.

Food: There's a market in Weaverville where you can stock up on food for the ride. Upon departing Weaverville you'll find no opportunities for food until Lewiston (mile 28), where the Lewiston Market has a limited selection. Back in Weaverville there are plenty of post-ride restaurants (Noelle's Garden Cafe has a great patio and garlicky gazpacho).

For more information: Ellison's Bicycle Shop, 105 Weaver Street, Weaverville, CA 96093; (530) 623-3377. Bring your mountain bike, too, if you can. There are endless miles of fire roads and single-track trails.

Maps: DeLorme *Northern California Atlas and Gazetteer*, map 45.

As you pass Trinity Dam, you begin the slow transition back to civilization, entering the narrow canyon that holds the emerald-green waters of Lewiston Lake. The lake is popular with boaters casting and trolling for finned creatures, and a host of campgrounds, RV parks, and boat launches line its shores. The vehicles that pass you here will likely have a recreational trailer of some kind in tow. Putting up with the trailer set is the small price that you pay for the vast improvement in road-surface quality, which turns from coarse tar and gravel to baby-butt-smooth asphalt along the lake shore.

A climb out of the Whiskeytown-Shasta-Trinity Recreation

Peaks tower above Rush Creek Road.

0.0 Take Highway 3 toward Trinity from Main Street (Highway 299) in downtown Weaverville; begin climbing out of town. Though the shoulder is good, be sure to watch out for RVs.

2.8 Summit.

5.0 Begin steeper climb.

6.5 Summit.

8.0 Right onto Trinity Dam Boulevard. Begin climbing.

10.4 Summit at Buckeye Ridge. Continue straight.

12.9 Enter Whiskeytown-Shasta-Trinity National Recreation Area.

13.2 Begin climbing again!

14.5 Summit.

16.5 Trinity vista overlook. Begin steep descent.

19.2 Trinity Dam vista.

20.5 Pass Pine Cove Marina and Boat Ramp.

25.0 Copper Gulch Campground. Begin another climb.

25.9 Summit.

27.2 Leave Whiskeytown-Shasta-Trinity National Recreation Area.

27.8 Straight past Rush Creek Road and the sign to Weaverville.

27.9 Right onto Deadwood Road.

28.0 Lewiston.

28.8 Right onto Turnpike Road over old bridge.

29.0 Left onto Rush Creek Road. Begin climbing.

30.0 Summit.

34.0 Begin climbing.

37.6 Left onto Highway 3 to Weaverville.

38.1 Summit.

43.4 Weaverville city limits.

44.8 Ride ends at Main Street (Highway 299) in Weaverville.

Area brings you to the outskirts of Lewiston. Another historic mining town, this curious little settlement has few amenities. You'll find a hotel, a few antiques shops, a market, a B&B, and little else.

From Lewiston the route follows Rush Creek Road. Though it is more heavily traveled than the boulevard, the traffic is still relatively light. There's one more extended climb that seems harder than it should be—perhaps because you're almost home, perhaps because you've been climbing for hours. After reaching the top, pedal 7 more miles and you're back to Highway 3, which features a long, luscious descent back into Weaverville.

Mad River Challenge

ARCATA — FRESHWATER — MAD RIVER —
BLUE LAKE — ARCATA

*S*ome *rides are leisurely and flat; others are not. This ride clearly falls into the latter category. With considerable climbing through the steep Arcata outback and Mad River, this challenge is one heck of a thigh burner. If you're looking for a good workout, you'll find it here. You'll also find some incredible ridge-top scenery that includes sparkling views of Humboldt Bay, the silver-blue Pacific, and endless green forested hills. Most of the roads on this route are lightly traveled, though there are those pesky logging trucks to contend with. Don't hesitate to pull over before they rumble up behind you.*

With its palm trees and grassy open space, Arcata's downtown plaza is reminiscent of Southern California, though the granola culture is nothing like that of L.A. Beyond the plaza the woodsy ambiance of the surrounding countryside takes hold. From Arcata's outer neighborhoods you roll past big barns and grassy cow pastures. The traffic can be fast to the town of Freshwater, and the shoulder is narrow or nonexistent, so take care. After mile 9 the trees close in, and you're soon climbing up a narrow serpentine road that takes you into deep forest.

The first climb lasts for only 2 miles, before being interrupted by a brief descent. But soon you're climbing again and quickly make up the lost elevation. As you ascend, you turn onto Kneeland Road and then later onto Butler Valley Road. With each turn you get farther away from civilization, until you eventually descend and cross the Mad River at mile 24.1. It is wise to take it easy on the descents, as the bumps and craters can make quick work of even the

Start: Arcata Plaza, Ninth and H Streets in downtown Arcata.

Length: 49 miles.

Terrain: Very hilly, with few flat sections. Road is in poor shape, with many dangerous potholes.

Food: Stock up on food in Arcata, as there's nothing until Blue Lake. Arcata's Wildberries is a good source for healthful snacks you can pack in your jersey for the ride.

For more information: Henderson Center Bike Shop, 2811 F Street, Eureka, CA 95501; (701) 443–7827. Life Cycle Bicycles, Fifteenth and G Streets, Arcata, CA 95521; (707) 822–7755.

Maps: DeLorme *Northern California Atlas and Gazetteer*, maps 42 and 43.

strongest wheels. There are also several long sections where the pavement gives way entirely to dirt.

After Mad River, that's right, you are climbing again. This time the climb lasts about 2.5 miles before the first summit reprieve. After that it's up and down and up and down on some chewed-up tarmac, which barely meets the definition. Finally, at mile 34.7 the undulations stop, and a long, bumpy descent leads you to the town of Blue Lake.

The first thing you'll see as you get out of the woods and cross the north fork of the Mad River is a sawmill. You can get a snack or drink at the Blue Lake food mart to ward off the bonk. After riding through the sleepy town center, you cross the Mad River and cruise along a beautiful, narrow country road. Along the way you'll pass a turnoff for the local fish hatchery, which is always worth a brief stop to ogle the lunkers. The last few miles through Arcata take you past yet another sawmill (beware of the diagonal railroad tracks; always cross them perpendicularly) and lead you safely back to the land of tie-dye and tofu.

Cud action in the Freshwater Valley.

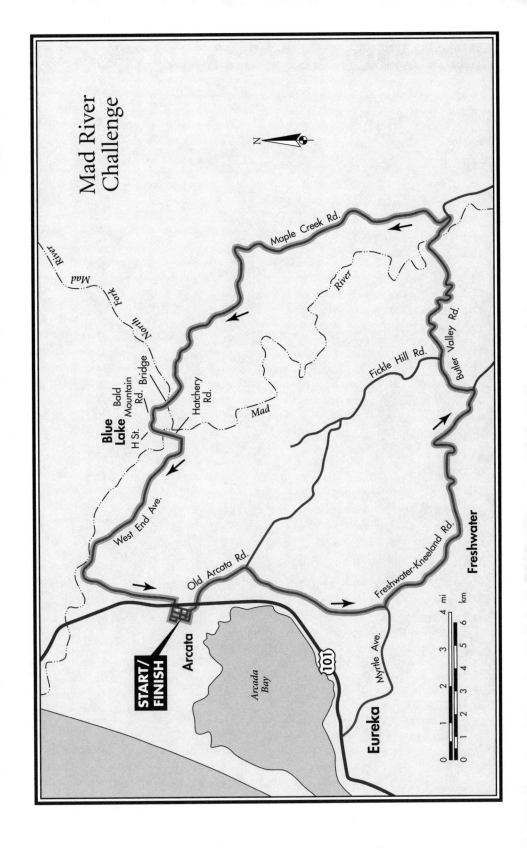

0.0 Head south on H Street from the Arcata Plaza.

0.2 Left onto Samoa Boulevard.

0.3 Cross over Highway 101 overpass.

0.6 Veer right at roundabout. (Bike trail begins just before roundabout on right.)

1.1 Samoa Boulevard becomes Old Arcata Road.

4.8 Old Arcata Road becomes Myrtle Avenue at Indianola Road cutoff.

7.5 Left onto Freshwater-Kneeland Road. Enter Freshwater.

9.3 Enter redwood-fir forest.

12.6 Begin climb (switchbacks).

13.1 Views of Humboldt Bay.

13.7 Left onto Kneeland Road.

15.2 Summit. Begin descending.

17.6 Left onto Butler Valley Road.

19.3 Pass Fickle Hill Road.

23.5 Views of peaks to east and south.

24.1 Cross Mad River bridge. Begin climbing.

25.1 Left onto Maple Creek Road toward Blue Lake.

26.7 Summit. Begin descending.

26.9 Begin climbing.

27.5 Summit. Begin descending.

28.8 Begin climbing.

31.1 Summit.

31.2 Cross creek bridge. Begin climbing.

33.2 Summit.

34.5 Veer left toward Blue Lake (Bald Mountain Road merge). Begin steep descent.

37.0 Cross bridge over North Fork of Mad River. Pass by sawmill.

38.4 Left onto Railroad Avenue. Enter town of Blue Lake.

39.0 Left onto H Street and 100 yards later left onto Hatchery Road.

39.4 Cross bridge over Mad River.

44.9 Right onto West End Avenue.

46.5 Begin paralleling Highway 101.

46.9 Bear right at roundabout onto Spear Avenue.

47.2 Left onto Alliance Road.

48.5 Left onto Twelfth Street.

48.8 Right onto H Street.

49.0 Ride ends at Arcata Plaza.

Central Coast

Lake Nacimiento Classic

PASO ROBLES — LAKE NACIMIENTO — SAN ANTONIO
RESERVOIR — LOCKWOOD — PASO ROBLES

Paso Robles may not exactly be the place you'd want to spend a monthlong vacation, but there is good biking value in the surrounding environs, and it's worth a weekend trip. The Lake Nacimiento Classic rolls into the unexplored farmland of the Central Coast, an area with many backroads and few cars. This tough but inspiring ride will purge both your soul and, should you fail to stay properly fueled, your muscles of their last drop of glycogen (water, too). Also keep in mind that it is often extremely hot here, and shade is a precious commodity, making early spring and late fall the best times to plan a ride.

The road out to Lake Nacimiento, the first leg of the trip, with many climbs, is popular among cyclists. But not all go for the full loop. To make this ride a cruise instead of a classic, you could head out to the lake, do some recreating, and then simply turn around and head back to Paso Robles. If you continue on from the Lake Nacimiento Resort, North Shore, you'll be faced with a steep climb that eventually drops you down into vast tableland. You probably won't run into too many other bicyclists out here.

Though it remains a lonely place, Lake Nacimiento has been increasingly settled in recent years. You'll pass by large hillside estates bordered by long white fences, behind which a few horses may be grazing. But the folks in the houses don't seem to get out much, and most of the traffic you encounter will be headed toward the lake and reservoir.

As you near Lockwood at mile 40.3, you transition from the open plains to fertile, tree-covered hills. After nearly 12 miles of tough climbs, you are treated

The glasslike surface of Lake Nacimiento.

to incredible views from high above the San Antonio Reservoir, which sparkles below and marks your return back to Paso Robles.

From the reservoir you're once again on the undulations of Nacimiento Lake Drive, and you can glide back to town tired from the long miles and tough climbs but refueled both mentally and physically.

THE BASICS

Start: Paso Robles (off Highway 101) at Twenty-fourth and Spring Streets.

Length: 80 miles.

Terrain: Hilly; steep climbs; some extended flat areas. Open roads; little traffic except for Nacimiento Lake Drive and G–18. Expect high heat during summer (and possibly late spring and early fall) with very little shade.

Food: Stock up in Paso Robles; otherwise, you're limited to a store in Lockwood at mile 40.3 or the Bee Rock store at mile 57.9.

For more information: San Luis Obispo Bike Club; www.slobc.org or (805) 543–5973. Sunstorm Cyclery, 6905 El Camino Real, Atascadero, CA 93422; (805) 466–6430.

Maps: DeLorme *Southern and Central California Atlas and Gazetteer,* maps 44 and 45; Compass Maps, *San Luis Obispo County.*

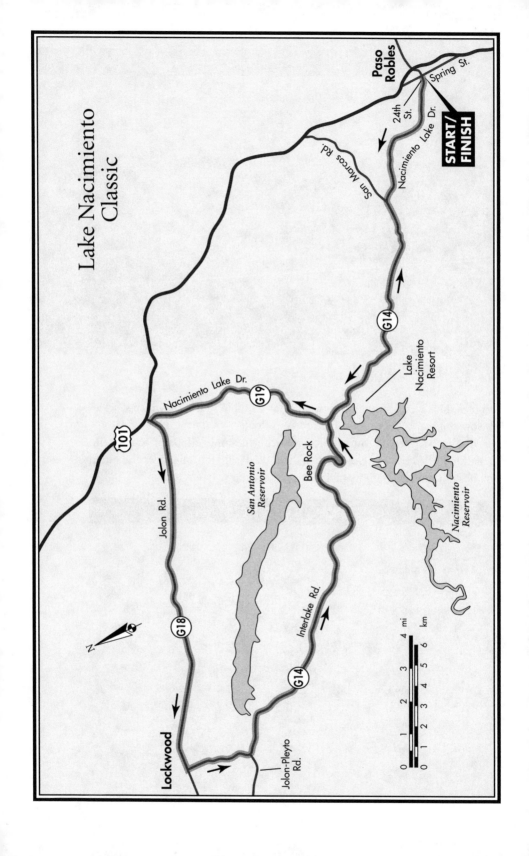

0.0 From Twenty-fourth and Spring Streets, go west on Twenty-fourth Street.

0.4 Veer right, following Nacimiento Lake Drive.

6.1 Straight past San Marcos Road.

8.1 Right onto G–14, Nacimiento Lake Drive.

8.2 Begin climb.

9.2 Summit.

15.8 Right, following G–14 to Lake Nacimiento/San Antonio Reservoir Recreation Area.

16.2 Lake Nacimiento Resort, North Shore. Begin steep climb.

17.2 Summit.

17.5 Straight past Interlake Road, following G–19, Nacimiento Lake Drive.

19.3 Veer right, following Nacimiento Lake Drive.

26.4 Left onto G–18, Jolon (pronounced hoh-lon) Road.

35.5 Straight past Jolon-Pleyto Road.

40.3 Lockwood city limits.

41.7 Left onto G–14, Interlake Road.

48.2 Begin climb.

49.2 Summit.

54.7 Begin climb.

55.7 Summit.

57.9 Bee Rock Store.

59.2 Begin climb.

60.8 Summit.

62.5 Right onto G–14, Nacimiento Lake Drive.

79.6 Nacimiento Lake Drive becomes Twenty-fourth Street.

80.0 Ride ends at Twenty-fourth and Spring Streets.

San Luis Valley Cruise

SAN LUIS OBISPO — ARROYO GRANDE — GROVER BEACH —
PISMO BEACH — EDNA — SAN LUIS OBISPO

I*n San Luis Obispo, city and country rub elbows. It's the kind of place where you can ride from the busy, rambunctious streets to serene roads in less than ten minutes. And don't think cyclists haven't figured this out. As soon as you roll out of town, you'll find yourself shar- ing the road with more bikes than cars.*

Your ride starts on the heavily trafficked streets of downtown San Luis Obispo before heading out to the more countrified Orcutt Road, which weaves

THE BASICS

Start: Downtown San Luis Obispo, accessible via Highway 101.

Length: 32.6 miles.

Terrain: Rolling hills; quiet roads interspersed with busy sections in city.

Food: There's a health-food store in Pismo Beach. There are also plenty of options at the ride start/finish in San Luis Obispo.

For more information: San Luis Obispo Bike Club; www.slobc.org or (805) 543–5973. Art's Cyclery, 2140 Santa Barbara Street, San Luis Obispo, CA 93401; (805) 543–4416.

Maps: DeLorme *Southern and Central California Atlas and Gazetteer*, map 59; Compass Maps, *San Luis Obispo County.*

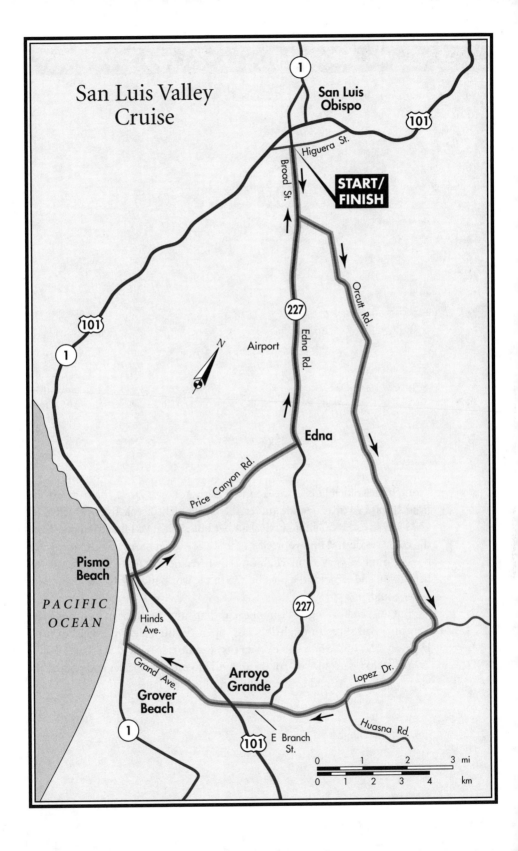

San Luis Valley Cruise

San Luis Obispo

START/FINISH

Higuera St.

Broad St.

Orcutt Rd.

(1)

(101)

(101)

(227)

Airport

Edna Rd.

Edna

Price Canyon Rd.

Pismo Beach

PACIFIC OCEAN

Hinds Ave.

Grand Ave.

Grover Beach

Arroyo Grande

(227)

Lopez Dr.

(1)

(101)

E Branch St.

Huasna Rd.

| 0 | 1 | 2 | 3 mi |
| 0 | 1 | 2 | 3 | 4 | km |

0.0 From Higuera Street and Broad Street, go left (south) on Broad Street.

1.5 Left onto Orcutt Road.

2.3 Veer right at stop sign, following Orcutt Road.

3.3 Left at stop sign, following Orcutt Road.

10.9 Lopez Water Treatment Plant.

11.5 Right onto Lopez Drive to Arroyo Grande.

14.2 Straight past Huasna Road to Arroyo Grande.

15.0 Arroyo Grande city limits. Lopez Drive becomes Huasna Road.

15.8 Left onto Stanley; road becomes East Branch Street.

16.1 Downtown Arroyo Grande.

16.8 Cross Highway 101; road becomes Grand Avenue.

19.5 Right onto Highway 1.

21.0 Right onto Hinds Avenue.

21.2 Cross Highway 101; road becomes Price Canyon Road. This stretch of road is narrow and can be fairly busy.

26.1 Left onto Highway 227 to San Luis Obispo.

29.5 San Luis Obispo airport.

30.7 San Luis Obispo city limits. Highway 227 intersects with Orcutt; becomes Broad Street.

32.6 Ride ends at Broad Street and Higuera Street.

through the golden hills of the Central Coast. At Lopez Drive you turn left and head toward Arroyo Grande under the shade of lush oak trees, which soon gives way to the area's more typical amber hills. When you finally emerge from the countryside and find yourself in the seaside town of Arroyo Grande, you'll be just 4 miles away from Highway 1, where the Pacific Ocean spreads out before you and expands the possibilities of the world in a way those inland hills never could.

But after a short jog to Pismo Beach, your route heads back inland as Price Canyon Road slices through the vast, open countryside. And when you hit Highway 227, you're home free on an easy 6-mile ride back to San Luis Obispo. There you can patronize one of the myriad hip eateries or cafes and ponder the virtues of both city and country while sipping your latte.

38

Cambria Challenge

CAMBRIA — MORRO STRAND STATE BEACH — CAYUCOS —
OLD CREEK ROAD — WHALE ROCK RESERVOIR — CAMBRIA

I f you've seen Arachnophobia, *you may recall the all-American town beset by the movie's dreaded monster. That was Cambria. The town's other claim to fame is its location 7 miles south of Hearst Castle. Beyond that, this former ranching center, just inland of the Central California coast, has retained much of its sleepy airs.*

For cyclists the Cambria Challenge serves as a benchmark (or brunchmark—this place is also known for its olallieberry pies and pancakes) of physical challenge and natural beauty. You will feel both exhausted and exhilarated by completing this loop. As the terrain keeps you pumping, the changing landscape offers a panoply of breathtaking views. There's a new reward for every crested summit, a payback for every mile completed.

After warming up on the mile-long climb out of town (perhaps heavy under an olallieberry load), this challenge heads south along Highway 1. Though traffic can

Mustard blooms on the roadside in the Santa Lucia Range.

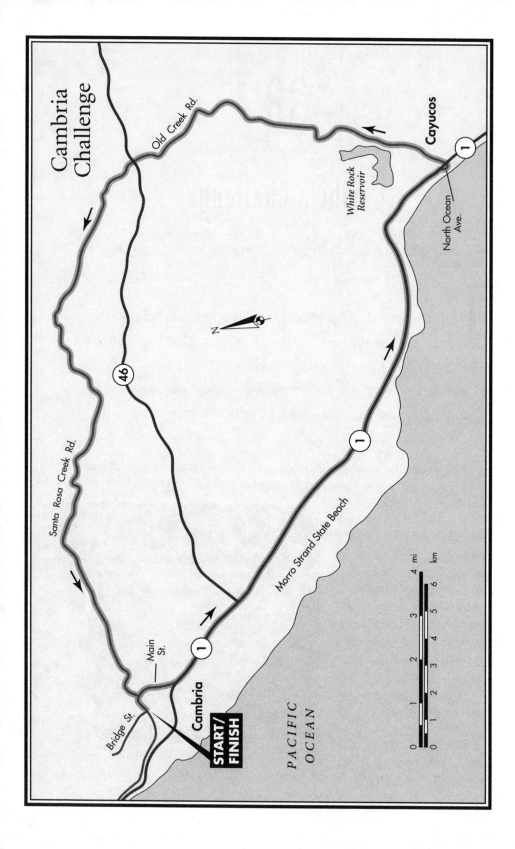

be steady here, the wide, wide shoulder is more than adequate. If it feels as though you've sprouted wings, thank the usually north-to-south prevailing wind, which will make the 13 miles to Cayucos slip by with surprising brevity. Along the way the closed-in grassy hills you've been riding through will suddenly open to the long rocky coast of Morro Strand State Beach, where it usually gets noticeably cooler. In the distance, if the fog is not too thick, you may see the somewhat dark, sinister form of "the Rock."

After a quick jaunt through the unpretentious working-class town of Cayucos, you turn east on Old Creek Road, leaving most of the traffic behind and beginning the first in a series of climbs through the Santa Lucia Range. As you ascend, you'll pass Whale Rock Reservoir, popular with anglers, and then descend past cottonwood trees to a lovely orange grove (thick with the scent of blossoms in spring), before tackling another long and occasionally steep climb to the summit. It can be interminably hot on the inland climbs, with minimal shade. As you sweat the hills to the summit, in the distance you may see fog creeping inland off Morro Bay, a promise of cooler temperatures to come.

THE BASICS

Start: Main and Bridge Streets, Cambria (East Village).

Length: 43.0 miles.

Terrain: Two major climbs; steep descent; rolling with some flats. Lightly traveled, with the exception of 12 miles on Highway 1.

Food: Robin's in Cambria serves extraordinary lunches and dinners. Linn's does a "berry" good breakfast.

For more information: Cambria Chamber of Commerce, 767 Main Street (West Village), Cambria, CA 93428, Phone (805) 927-3624. Cambria Bicycle Outfitter, 2164 Center Street, Cambria, CA 93428; (805) 927-5510.

Maps: Compass Maps, *San Luis Obispo County.*

The road then plunges down and rolls for a bit before crossing Highway 46. If you are too tired to go on (there's still a challenging climb ahead), you can exit the ride here by taking Highway 46 back to Highway 1 and Cambria. But you will miss some of the best this loop has to offer.

From here the route is lightly traveled and winds through oak chaparral lined with a wonderful array of mustard, wild pink pea, and purple lupine that bloom brilliantly in spring. The road itself is paved in silver-gray stone and has a fresh, clean look about it. At mile 29 you begin a climb up a particularly nasty pitch that will make you wish for your granny (the chain-ring variety). At the summit you'll be treated with a view that includes a good part of the upcoming descent. It looks as if it goes on forever—and almost does (there is one more short climb hidden out there). But beware, the road is exceedingly bumpy and includes an asphalt ledge or two, probably the result of some fault line. If taken at speed, the ledges will send you over the bars.

MILES AND DIRECTIONS

0.0 Head south on Main Street from intersection with Bridge Street.

0.4 Begin climbing.

1.5 Summit. Left onto Highway 1 at traffic light.

13.5 Right onto North Ocean Avenue toward Cayucos.

15.3 Ocean Avenue merges with Highway 1.

16.3 Left onto Old Creek Road (through small residential area). Begin climbing.

19.4 Summit. Begin long descent.

20.4 Bottom of hill. Begin climb.

23.9 Summit. Begin descending.

25.9 Intersection with Highway 46. Continue straight and begin climbing.

26.5 Summit. Begin descent.

26.8 Bottom of descent.

29.0 Begin climbing (steep at times).

29.8 Summit. Begin long and, at times, extremely rough descent.

32.5 Begin paralleling stream in park.

42.4 Right on Main Street.

43.0 End at Bridge and Main Streets.

You'll know you're getting close to Cambria as the air takes on a familiar, almost feverish, chill from the sea. Five miles outside of town you'll pass Linn's Farms, the source of the olallieberries (their restaurant in town goes by the same name), where you can purchase an assortment of goodies.

Now the question and answer you've been waiting for: What is an olallieberry? It's a cross between a blackberry and a red raspberry. Enjoy!

Morro Bay Ramble

MORRO BAY — LOS OSOS — MORRO BAY

Morro Rock rests on the edge of the Pacific like a huge monster washed ashore. Known as the "Gibraltar of the Pacific," the rock possesses a sinister beauty accentuated by the towering smokestacks of a nearby PG&E power plant. But that's not all. Morro is actually a volcano, part of a string of nine volcanic peaks stretching inland to San Luis Obispo. Overall Morro Rock makes for a surreal setting, particularly when all is enshrouded in fog.

Noir aspects aside, the Morro Bay Ramble is a delightful jaunt that takes you along a wildlife refuge and through green, fertile fields. Beginning on the outskirts of town, you ride out to Morro Rock Ecological Reserve State Park. Along the way you may see a seal basking in the sun or kayakers plying the still water of the bay. From there you continue through town along Embarcadero Street, where seafood restaurants, T-shirt shops, crowds, and the other trappings of tourism abound. (Beware of wayward tourists and car doors that open without warning as you attempt to pass.)

After town you'll continue on to Morro Bay State Park and the Black Hill Golf Course, with excellent views of the dunes and tidelands to the west. Notice the odd bike lane along Main Street before entering the park; it is actually a sidewalk-cum-bike-lane that courses up and down the ramps of residential driveways. Beware of incoming/outgoing traffic.

Reaching South Bay Boulevard, the fog should begin to disappear as you make your way around the Morro Bay Wildlife Refuge. South Bay Boulevard and the subsequent section on Los Osos Valley Road can be rife with vehicles,

Start: Junction of Highway 1 and Highway 41 (Atascadero Road) in Morro Bay. From Highway 1 take Atascadero, Highway 41 exit.

Length: 21.0 miles.

Terrain: Rolling hills; some short, steep pitches; many flat sections. Mostly quiet roads; some heavily trafficked sections on South Bay Boulevard, Los Osos Valley Road and in downtown Morro Bay. Beware of opening doors on parked cars.

Food: Myriad restaurants in Morro Bay, including the Great American Fish Company and Fat Cat's Cafe, both on Embarcadero Street.

For more information: San Luis Obispo Bike Club; www.slobc.org or (805) 543–5973. Baywood Cyclery, 2179 Tenth Street, Los Osos, CA 93402; (805) 528–5115.

Maps: DeLorme *Southern and Central California Atlas and Gazetteer,* map 59.

but a bike lane and a good shoulder give you an adequate berth. At mile 12 you turn onto exquisite Turri Road, which rolls gently upward through black-dirt farm country and beneath green-carpeted hills, slowly making its way back to Los Osos Valley Road and Morro Bay.

Morro Rock appears from the mist.

After the steep but short climb up to Black Hill Golf Course, you'll drop quickly into town. When you finish the ride in another 1.5 miles, you may find yourself heading back over to Embarcadero Street for some wharf-style seafood. And that just may be the perfect ending to your alternately sunny and surreal ride.

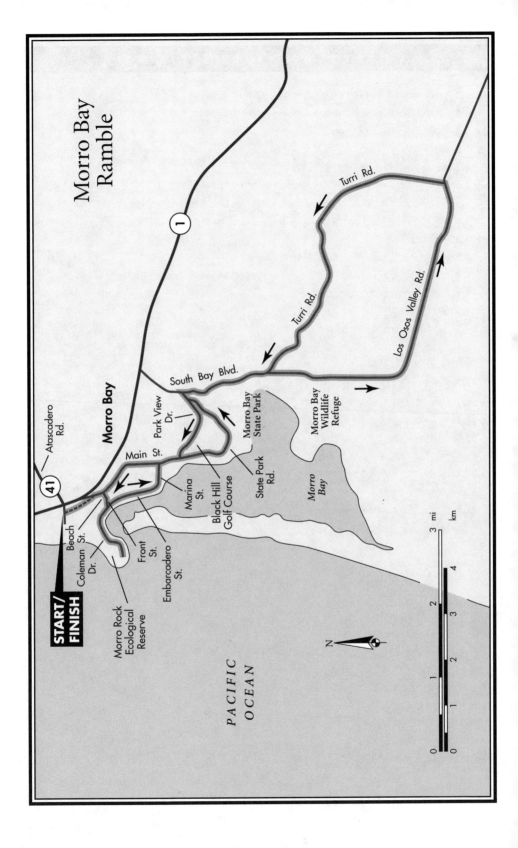

0.0 Head south on bike path from Atascadero Road.

0.5 Right onto Main Street and up short hill.

0.8 Right onto Beach Street.

1.0 Right onto Front Street.

1.2 Merge with Embarcadero Street.

1.4 Veer left onto Coleman Drive toward Morro Rock.

2.0 Road ends at parking lot; turn around and head back through town.

2.6 Veer right on Embarcadero Street.

3.3 Left onto Marina Street.

3.5 Right onto Main Street.

4.4 Enter Morrow Bay State Park (Main Street becomes State Park Road).

6.1 Right onto South Bay Boulevard.

9.3 Left onto Los Osos Vallery Road.

12.0 Left onto Turri Road.

13.0 Road curves sharply left and begins climbing up.

14.0 Summit.

16.7 Right onto South Bay Boulevard.

18.0 Left into Morrow Bay State Park.

18.2 Right onto Park View Drive, climbing up to Black Hill Golf Course.

18.8 Summit and golf course.

19.1 Right at stop sign onto Main Street.

20.5 Intersection with Highway 1. Cross Main Street to bike path around power plant.

21.0 End at Atascadero Road.

Hunter Liggett Challenge

FORT HUNTER LIGGETT MILITARY RESERVATION —
BIG SUR — FORT HUNTER LIGGETT MILITARY RESERVATION

On the edge of the Ventana Wilderness and Los Padres National Forest, Fort Hunter Liggett Military Reservation occupies about 165,000 acres of largely undeveloped land on the east side of the Santa Lucia Mountains. Though it is an active U.S. Army installation (note the THREATCON LEVEL *sign posted at the entrance gate), its vast oak woodland, chaparral, and grassland plains remain largely untouched. In springtime the area has some of the best wild-flower displays around, including many rare plant species. It is also the site of Mission San Antonio, founded in 1771 by Padre Junipero Serra. This peaceful old Spanish mission is currently maintained by Franciscan friars as a parish church, retreat center, and historical site.*

The ride starts at the fort headquarters on Mission Road, near Mission San Antonio, and consists of two out-and-back rides through the upland valleys of the Santa Lucias. We treat these as two separate rides since they pass through the same starting point.

The first ride starts on Del Venturi Road and immediately fords the San Antonio River on a shallow paved ford. Don't be tempted to ride here, as the middle is slippery, and the current is just strong enough to sweep your wheels out from under you. It's better to remove your shoes and walk across. On a hot summer day, the walk will be refreshing.

Del Venturi gradually climbs through an oak chaparral until there is another paved ford of the San Antonio River. After the ford, you leave Fort Hunter

Start: Fort Hunter Liggett, Mission Road and Del Venturi Road. Fort Hunter Liggett can be reached on Jolon Road from King City. Call (831) 386–2503 to make sure all the roads in the fort are open.

Length: 38.0 miles and 34.0 miles.

Terrain: Gradual climbing on Del Venturi Road and Milpitas Road. Some cattle grates and cattle. Very little traffic. Two river fords. Somewhat more traffic on Nacimiento Fergusson Road. Steep climbing to the ridge at Cone Peak Road. Steep descending.

Food: Bring your own food and water. There is (generally) water at Ponderosa Campground.

For more information: Fort Hunter Liggett road-closure information, (831) 386–2503. Los Padres National Forest Service, (831) 385–5434. Hunter Liggett Campground, (831) 386–2550.

Maps: DeLorme *Southern and Central California Atlas and Gazetteer*, maps 44, 32, and 31.

Liggett and enter the Los Padres National Forest. The road starts seriously climbing. Be aware that you are now crossing open range. Ornery-looking cattle may be lounging along—and sometimes on—the road. Give them a wide berth.

With more climbing (to around 2,200 feet), you reach "The Indians," an area where Indians farmed in the late missionary period. This area features a large sandstone outcropping known as Wagon Cave. Across the road is Junipero Serra, the tallest peak in the Santa Lucias, at 5,844 feet.

A brief descent brings the route to the turnaround at the end of the paved road. This is Memorial Campground, a Forest Service campground where there is no drinking water. Beyond are 18 miles of dirt road, rough but ridable by intrepid road bikers (with sturdy tires). If you're interested in a truly epic loop, consider taking this route all the way to Carmel, with a return through Big Sur on Highway 1—a 150-mile sojourn that warrants several days of travel.

Statue of Father Junipero Serra at Mission San Antonio.

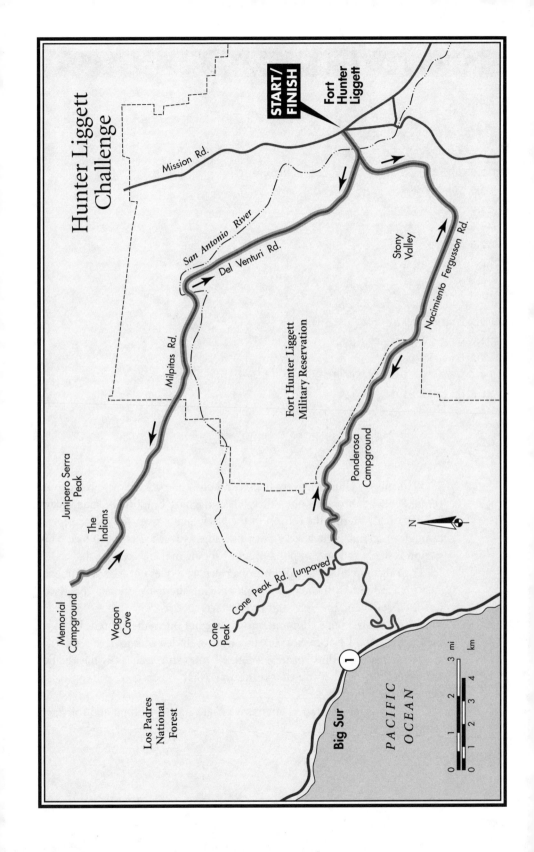

Hunter Liggett Challenge

START/FINISH

Fort Hunter Liggett

Mission Rd.

San Antonio River

Del Venturi Rd.

Milpitas Rd.

Stony Valley

Nacimiento Fergusson Rd.

Fort Hunter Liggett Military Reservation

Junipero Serra Peak

The Indians

Memorial Campground

Wagon Cave

Ponderosa Campground

Cone Peak Rd. (unpaved)

Cone Peak

Los Padres National Forest

N

Big Sur

PACIFIC OCEAN

1

3 mi

km

0   1   2   3

0   1   2   3   4

RIDE 1:

0.0 Mission Road and Del Venturi Road. Parking is available at the fort headquarters. Follow Del Venturi.

0.5 Ford of San Antonio River. Slippery!

7.0 Second ford of San Antonio River. Slippery!

8.0 Left on Milpitas Road.

12.0 Enter Los Padres National Forest.

16.0 The Indians, Wagon Cave.

19.0 Memorial Campground. Turn around.

RIDE 2:

0.0 Mission Road and Del Venturi Road. Parking is available at the fort headquarters. Follow Del Venturi.

0.5 Ford of San Antonio River. Slippery!

1.0 Left on Nacimiento Fergusson Road.

5.0 Stony Valley.

9.5 Leave Hunter Liggett; enter Los Padres National Forest.

10.5 Ponderosa Campground; water.

17.0 Reach summit at Cone Peak Road. Turn around. It is 7.0 miles and 2,000 feet down Nacimiento Fergusson Road to Highway 1.

Returning to Hunter Liggett, the second out-and-back follows Nacimiento Fergusson Road through Stony Valley, one of the most beautiful isolated valleys in California. Entering the canyon of the Nacimiento River, the road steepens through numerous switchbacks until the ridge is reached at 2,000 feet. This section is shady and wet, with many oaks hanging over the road.

The ridge top offers the adventurous rider, who does not wish to immediately turn around, with two difficult but enticing alternatives. First, Cone Peak Road, a dirt road on the right, climbs 1,500 feet toward Cone Peak (5,155 feet). This is a very strenuous climb on a road bike but offers magnificent views of the Pacific. Second, Nacimiento Fergusson abruptly descends to the ocean, with several decreasing radius corners, where all you can see ahead is the Pacific, 1,000 feet below. And, if you choose this way, what you descend, you must also climb on the return.

Finally, there is the easiest alternative: You can turn around and roll back toward your starting point.

Appendix

RECOMMENDED READING

A surprising amount of literature is devoted to the sport of cycling. The following titles and listings only begin to scratch the surface of what's out there, but they do provide a good starting place for learning more about the various aspects of the sport. To really hook into California's vast cycling network in three easy steps, you should (1) join a local cycling club or advocacy coalition; (2) read *Cycle California!* religiously; and (3) plan to complete at least one organized cycling event this year.

Regional Cycling Magazines

Cycle California!
P.O. Box 189
Mountain View, CA 94042
(650) 961–2663
www.cyclecalifornia.com

Cycle California!, the successor publication to *California Bicyclist*, is the end-all-be-all source for bicycling news, events, and information in California. *Cycle California!* publishes a complete calendar of events that is invaluable to anyone interested in cycling—recreational, touring, racing, or otherwise. You can get the magazine free at most bike shops, or you can purchase a subscription for $15.

NCNCA Newsletter
9320 Village Tree Drive
Elk Grove, CA 95878
www.ncnca.org

Devoted exclusively to racing, the *Northern California/Nevada Cycling Association Newsletter* is available in a few selected bike shops. It is the only source for the complete racing calendar, road and off-road. Subscriptions are $15 a year.

Baker, Arnie. *Bicycling Medicine: Cycling Nutrition, Physiology, Injury, Prevention, and Treatment for Riders of All Levels.* Simon & Shuster, 1998.

Bodfish. *California Dream Cycling.* Bodfish Books, 1990. Bodfish, aka Chuck Elliot, has a special feel for the high country.

Bodfish. *Cycling the California Outback.* Bodfish Books, 1986. Bodfish, aka Chuck Elliot, really gets into the outback.

Coello, Dennis. *Roadside Guide to Bike Repair.* Warner Books, 1988.

Coello, Dennis. *Touring on Two Wheels.* Nick Lyons Books, 1989. Practical information on safe and trouble-free bike touring.

Forester, John. *Effective Cycling.* MIT Press, 1992. Tips for urban riding and for improving safe riding practices and skills.

Hershon, Maynard. *Tales from the Bike Shop.* Ten Speed Press. A collection of humorous short stories written by one of cycling's preeminent writers.

Jenkins, Mark. *Off the Map: Bicycling across Siberia.* William Morrow and Company, 1992. Eloquent and inspirational cycling travelogue—read this to renew your passion and enthusiasm for the sport.

Loher, George T. *The Wonderful Ride.* Harper Collins, 1978. The journal of an intrepid California cyclist who rode his "wheel" to New York City in 1895.

Pavelka, Ed. *Bicycling Magazine's Complete Book of Road Cycling.* Rodale Press, 1998.

Peterson, Grant, and John Kluge. *Road to Ride and Roads to Ride South.* Heyday Books, 1984. A detailed description of every climb in the greater Bay Area.

Reynolds, Jim. *The Outer Path: Finding My Way in Tibet.* Fair Oaks Publishing, 1992. Another great cycling travelogue.

Sloane, Eugene. *The Complete Book of Bicycling.* Simon & Schuster, 1995.

Sloane, Eugene. *Sloane's New Bicycle Maintenance Manual.* Simon & Schuster, 1991.

CYCLING MAPS

The following maps were indispensable tools in the making of this book. They are available from Krebs Cycle Products, P.O. Box 7337, Santa Cruz, CA 95061. Perhaps one day Krebs will have maps like these for the entire state!

- *California North Coast* bicycle touring map
- *Lake Tahoe and Gold Country* bicycle touring map
- *North San Francisco Bay and Wine Country* bicycle touring map
- *San Francisco Peninsula and Santa Cruz Mountains* mountain biking map
- *South San Francisco Bay and Monterey Bay Areas* bicycle touring map

Also valuable was the *Northern California Atlas and Gazetteer* published by DeLorme.

CYCLING CLUBS/COALITIONS

The easiest way to access cycling clubs is to check the *Cycle California!* Web page at www.cyclecalifornia.com. Most local clubs are volunteer-based, and contact numbers are subject to change. Below is a listing of a few of the more prominent clubs.

National Cycling Clubs

Adventure Cycling Association
P.O. Box 8308
Missoula, MT 59807
(406) 721–1776; (800) 755–2453
www.adv-cycling.org
National bike touring organization; publishes cycling maps.

League of American Bicyclists
1612 K Street, NW
Washington, DC 20006
(202) 822–1333
www.bikeleague.org

Regional Cycling Clubs

Almaden Cycle Touring Club
P.O. Box 7286
San Jose, CA 95150
Hotline: (408) 255–0298
www.actc.org
A South Bay touring club with 900 members. Promotes Tierra Bella Century.

Alto Velo
Al Williams
1785 Balsa
San Jose, CA 95124
www.altovelo.org
The largest USCF racing club in Northern California.

Bay Area Roaming Tandems
Hotline: (510) 803–0363
www.cruzers.com/~glennandpat/
The largest tandem club in Northern California.

Chico Velo Cycling Club
P.O. Box 2285
Chico, CA 95927
Hotline: (800) 482-2453
www.chicovelo.com
Promoter of the Chico Wildflower and many other rides.

Davis Bike Club
610 Third Street
Davis, CA 95616
Hotline: (530) 756–0186
A large touring and racing club. Promoter of the Davis Double.

Diablo Cyclists
P.O. Box 30263
Walnut Creek, CA 94598
www.diablocyclists.com
An active touring club.

Fremont Freewheelers
P.O. Box 1868
Fremont, CA 94538
www.fremontfreewheelers.org
A touring club with some racing. Promoter of the Prima-vera.

Fresno Cycling Club
P.O. Box 11531
Fresno, CA 93773
www.fresnocycling.com
A large touring club. Promoter of the Climb to Kaiser.

Grizzly Peak Cyclists
P.O. Box 9308
Berkeley, CA 94709
(510) 655–4211
www.GrizzlyPeakCyclists.org
A touring club. Promoter of the Grizzly Peak Century.

Sacramento Wheelmen
P.O. Box 19817
Sacramento, CA 95819
(916) 791–3426
www.sacwheelmen.org
A large touring and long-distance riding club.

Santa Cruz County Cycling Club
P.O. Box 8342
Santa Cruz, CA 95061
(831) 423–0829
www.santacruzcycling.org

Santa Rosa Cycling Club
P.O. Box 6008
Santa Rosa, CA 95406
Hotline: (707) 544–4803
www.srcc.com
A large touring and long-distance riding club. Promoter of the Terrible Two
and the Wine Country Century.

Valley Spokesmen
P.O. Box 2630
Dublin, CA 94568
(925) 828–5299
www.valleyspokesmen.org
A large touring and racing club with more than 700 members. Promoter of the
Hekaton, Cinderella, and the Wente Road Race.

Western Wheelers
P.O. Box 518
Palo Alto, CA 94302
www.westernwheelers.org
A large touring club. Promoter of the Sequoia.

California Bicycle Coalition
909 12th Street, Suite 114
Sacramento, CA 95814
www.calbike.org

East Bay Bike Coalition
P.O. Box 1736
Oakland, CA 94604
www.ebbc.org

Marin County Bicycle Coalition
P.O. Box 35
San Anselmo, CA 94979
www.bikeadelic.com/mcbc/

Regional Bicycle Advocacy
P.O. Box 10205
Oakland, CA 94610
(510) 452–1221
www.bayareabikes.org

San Francisco Bicycle Coalition
1095 Market Street, #215
San Francisco, CA 94103
(415) 431–2453
www.sfbike.org

About the Authors

John Nagiecki

A former Colorado ski instructor and bicycle racer, John Nagiecki has been in relentless pursuit of the ultimate bike ride since he took to the sidewalk at age two. He's pedaled across the western and eastern United States, through parts of Alaska, and around Europe. He was also the first cyclist ever to ride the 500-mile length of the Colorado Trail. His aspirations include meeting former U.S. Olympic Cycling Coach Eddy Borysewicz, who is believed to be a long-lost cousin.

John occupies his nonbiking hours with freelance writing, editing, and photography assignments. His work has appeared in the *Seattle Times, San Francisco Examiner, San Jose Mercury News, E Magazine, the Ecologist,* and other national and international publications. He coauthored *Insiders' Guide to California's Wine Country* (2001) by The Globe Pequot Press.

Kimberly Grob

The former editor of *California Bicyclist* magazine, Kimberly Grob has dabbled in many aspects of the sport, including touring, mountain-bike racing, triathlon, and bike commuting. She has contributed to many national magazines, including *Mountain Bike, Velo News, Women's Sports and Fitness, Backpacker, Inside Triathlon,* and *Triathlete.*

FALCON GUIDES®

From nature exploration to extreme adventure, FalconGuides lead you there. With more than 400 titles available, there is a guide for every outdoor activity and topic, including essential outdoor skills, field identification, trails, trips, and the best places to go in each state and region. Written by experts, each guidebook features detailed descriptions, maps, and advice that can enhance every outdoor experience.

You can count on FalconGuides to lead you to your favorite outdoor activities wherever you live or travel.

ROAD BIKING™

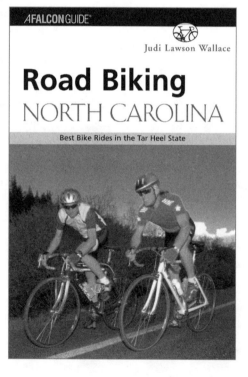

The routes in the Road Biking™ series are designed to provide great cycling in areas with little auto traffic and to showcase the state's natural and cultural landscapes along the way. The rides vary in length and difficulty from after-noon rambles anyone can enjoy to classic, multiday tours for the serious cyclist.

6" x 9" · 224 pp · photos and maps

A FALCON GUIDE®

Judi Lawson Wallace

Road Biking
NORTH CAROLINA

Best Bike Rides in the Tar Heel State